MEDITATION FOR BEGINNERS: A HOLISTIC APPROACH FOR SELF-IMPROVEMENT

WRITTEN BY ROSALIND BAKER

Printed by Draft2Digital
First printing, 2023.
Independent Publisher
Chicago, IL

Part I: Introduction

Understanding the definition of meditation is important for several reasons. Firstly, it helps to dispel common misconceptions about the practice. Meditation is often associated with religion or spirituality, and some people believe that it requires a specific set of beliefs or practices. However, the true definition of meditation is much broader and more inclusive than this. By understanding what meditation really is, individuals can come to see that it can be practiced by anyone, regardless of their religious or spiritual beliefs.

In addition, by understanding the definition of meditation, individuals can gain a clearer understanding of the purpose and benefits of the practice. There are many different types of meditation, each of which serves a different purpose. Some types of meditation are designed to promote relaxation and reduce stress, while others are intended to increase focus and concentration. By understanding the different types of meditation and their respective purposes, individuals can choose a practice that is best suited to their needs and goals.

Furthermore, understanding the definition of meditation can help individuals to better appreciate the complexity and depth of the practice. Meditation is not simply a way to clear the mind or achieve a state of relaxation. It is a multifaceted practice that has been studied and practiced for thousands of years. By understanding the nuances of meditation, individuals can approach the practice with a greater sense of respect and mindfulness.

Overall, understanding the definition of meditation is essential for anyone who wishes to practice the technique. By gaining a clear understanding of what meditation is and what it can do, individuals can approach the practice with greater knowledge, appreciation, and intentionality. Whether you are a seasoned practitioner or a beginner, understanding the definition of meditation is a critical step on the path to greater mindfulness and inner peace.

CHAPTER 1:
DEFINITION OF MEDITATION

Meditation is a practice that involves training the mind to focus on a particular object, thought, or activity with the goal of achieving a clear and calm state of mind. Meditation can be done in various ways, including sitting, standing, walking, or even lying down. The practice is often associated with mindfulness, which involves being aware of one's thoughts, feelings, and surroundings without judgment or distraction.

Meditation has been practiced for thousands of years in various cultures and religions around the world. Its origins can be traced back to ancient Hindu and Buddhist traditions, where it was used as a means of achieving spiritual enlightenment. The practice of meditation spread to other parts of the world, including China, Japan, and the Middle East, where it was integrated into various religious and philosophical traditions.

In recent years, meditation has gained popularity in the West as a means of reducing stress, improving concentration, and promoting overall well-being. It has been studied extensively by scientists and researchers, who have found that it can have a variety of physical and mental health benefits.

Different Types of Meditation:

There are many different types of meditation, each with its own unique techniques and benefits. Some of the most common types of meditation include:

1. Mindfulness meditation - this involves focusing on the present moment and observing one's thoughts and feelings without judgment.

2. Transcendental meditation - this involves repeating a mantra or sound to help the mind achieve a deep state of relaxation.

3. Loving-kindness meditation - this involves sending positive thoughts and emotions to oneself and others.

4. Vipassana meditation - this involves observing one's breath and bodily sensations to gain insight into the nature of reality.

5. Yoga meditation - this involves practicing yoga postures while focusing on breath and body awareness.

These are just a few examples of the many types of meditation that exist. Each type of meditation has its own benefits and can be practiced by anyone, regardless of their background or beliefs.

CHAPTER 2:
THE PURPOSE OF MEDITATION

Spiritual Purposes of Meditation:

Meditation has been used for thousands of years as a tool for spiritual growth and enlightenment. Many religious and spiritual traditions incorporate meditation into their practices, as it is believed to help individuals connect with a higher power or divine energy. Some of the spiritual purposes of meditation include:

1. Deepening one's connection to a higher power or divine energy
2. Cultivating a sense of inner peace and calm
3. Gaining insight into the nature of reality and the self
4. Developing greater compassion and empathy for others
5. Achieving a state of spiritual enlightenment or transcendence

Physical Purposes of Meditation:

In addition to its spiritual benefits, meditation has also been shown to have a variety of physical benefits. When practiced regularly, meditation can promote overall health and well-being by reducing stress, improving sleep quality, and lowering blood pressure. Some of the physical purposes of meditation include:

1. Reducing stress and anxiety
2. Improving sleep quality and duration
3. Lowering blood pressure and reducing the risk of heart disease
4. Boosting the immune system

5. Relieving pain and inflammation

Psychological Purposes of Meditation:

Finally, meditation has a wide range of psychological benefits, particularly when it comes to promoting mental health and emotional well-being. Regular meditation practice has been shown to reduce symptoms of depression and anxiety, improve focus and concentration, and increase feelings of happiness and contentment. Some of the psychological purposes of meditation include:

1. Reducing symptoms of anxiety and depression

2. Improving focus and concentration

3. Increasing feelings of happiness and contentment

4. Developing greater self-awareness and emotional regulation

5. Enhancing overall psychological well-being and resilience.

Meditation serves a wide range of purposes, from spiritual growth to physical health and psychological well-being. By practicing meditation regularly, individuals can experience a variety of benefits that can improve their overall quality of life.

How Meditation Works

The Science of Meditation:

Meditation is a practice that involves training the mind to focus on a particular object or thought, while letting go of distractions and negative thoughts. While the practice of meditation has been around for thousands of years, recent scientific research has shed light on how it works and the benefits it can provide.

The Effects of Meditation on the Brain

Research has shown that meditation can have a significant impact on the brain, particularly in areas related to attention, emotional regulation, and cognitive processing. For example, studies have found that regular meditation practice can increase the thickness of the prefrontal cortex, which is involved in decision-making and self-awareness. Other research has shown that meditation can increase activity in the amygdala, which is involved in emotional regulation and response. Overall, these changes in the brain can lead to improved focus, reduced stress and anxiety, and greater emotional stability.

The Effects of Meditation on the Body:

In addition to its effects on the brain, meditation can also have a significant impact on the body. Research has shown that regular meditation practice can reduce the levels of stress hormones such as cortisol and adrenaline, which can have a range of benefits for physical health. For example, lower levels of stress hormones can lead to lower blood pressure, reduced inflammation, and improved immune function. Meditation has also been shown to improve sleep quality, which can have a positive impact on overall health and well-being.

Meditation works by training the mind to focus on a particular object or thought, while letting go of distractions and negative thoughts. This practice can lead to a range of benefits for both the brain and the body, including improved focus, reduced stress and anxiety, and better physical health.

Techniques of Meditation

Meditation is a practice that involves training the mind to focus on a particular object or thought, while letting go of distractions and negative thoughts. There are several different techniques of meditation, each with its own unique approach and benefits. Here are three common techniques of meditation:

Mindfulness Meditation:

Mindfulness meditation involves focusing on the present moment, without judgment or distraction. This technique involves paying attention to the sensations in the body, the breath, and the thoughts and feelings that arise, observing them without getting caught up in them. Mindfulness meditation is often used to reduce stress and anxiety, increase focus and self-awareness, and improve emotional regulation.

Transcendental Meditation:

Transcendental meditation is a technique that involves using a mantra or sound to focus the mind and achieve a state of deep relaxation. This technique is often practiced twice a day for 20 minutes at a time, and is said to lead to a range of benefits, including reduced stress, improved focus and creativity, and increased energy and vitality.

Loving-Kindness Meditation:

Loving-kindness meditation involves focusing on feelings of love, compassion, and kindness towards oneself and others. This technique involves visualizing oneself and others, and sending positive thoughts and intentions towards them. Loving-kindness meditation is often used to increase feelings of empathy and connection, reduce negative emotions such as anger and resentment, and cultivate a sense of inner peace and well-being.

Overall, there are many different techniques of meditation, each with its own unique approach and benefits. By practicing one or more of these techniques regularly, individuals can improve their mental and physical health, reduce stress and anxiety, and cultivate a greater sense of inner peace and well-being.

CHAPTER 3:
BENEFITS OF MEDITATION

Meditation is a practice that has been used for thousands of years to promote relaxation, reduce stress, and improve overall well-being. While there are many different techniques of meditation, they all share a common goal of training the mind to focus and become more aware. Here are three different categories of benefits that meditation can provide:

Meditation has been shown to have a range of physical benefits, including:

- Reduced inflammation and pain: Meditation has been shown to reduce inflammation and pain in individuals with a range of conditions, including arthritis, fibromyalgia, and chronic back pain.

- Lowered blood pressure: Meditation has been shown to reduce blood pressure in individuals with hypertension, leading to a decreased risk of heart disease and stroke.

- Improved sleep: Meditation can help improve sleep quality and reduce insomnia, leading to increased energy and improved overall health.

- Reduced symptoms of illness: Meditation has been shown to reduce symptoms of a range of illnesses, including asthma, irritable bowel syndrome, and psoriasis.

Meditation has also been shown to have a range of mental benefits, including:

- Reduced stress and anxiety: Meditation can help reduce stress and anxiety by promoting relaxation and reducing negative thoughts and emotions.

- Improved focus and concentration: Meditation can help improve focus and concentration, leading to increased productivity and better decision-making.

- Increased self-awareness: Meditation can help individuals become more aware of their thoughts, emotions, and behaviors, leading to improved self-awareness and a greater sense of personal growth.

- Reduced symptoms of depression: Meditation can help reduce symptoms of depression by promoting positive emotions and reducing negative thought patterns.

Meditation can also have a range of spiritual benefits, including:

- Increased feelings of inner peace and well-being: Meditation can help individuals cultivate a sense of inner peace and well-being, leading to a greater sense of happiness and fulfillment.

- Greater connection to a higher power: Meditation can help individuals feel more connected to a higher power or spiritual source, leading to a greater sense of purpose and meaning in life.

- Increased compassion and empathy: Meditation can help individuals cultivate feelings of compassion and empathy towards others, leading to improved relationships and a greater sense of community.

Overall, meditation can provide a wide range of benefits for both the mind and body. By practicing meditation regularly, individuals can experience improved physical health, reduced stress and anxiety, and a greater sense of connection to themselves and others.

Misconceptions About Meditation

Meditation is a practice that has been around for thousands of years and has gained popularity in recent years due to its numerous benefits for the mind and body. However, there are still many misconceptions about meditation that prevent people from trying it or taking it seriously. Here are three common misconceptions about meditation:

Meditation is not a religion:

One of the biggest misconceptions about meditation is that it is a religious practice. While meditation may be a part of some religious traditions, it is not inherently a religious practice. Meditation is simply a technique for training the mind and improving focus and awareness. People from all different backgrounds and belief systems can practice meditation and benefit from it.

Meditation is not a way to escape reality:

Another common misconception about meditation is that it is a way to escape reality or avoid problems. In reality, meditation is a way to become more present and aware of one's thoughts and emotions. By practicing mindfulness, individuals can learn to observe their thoughts and emotions without judgment, leading to greater insight and understanding of themselves and their experiences. This can help individuals better cope with difficult emotions and situations, rather than avoiding them.

Meditation is not a quick fix:

Finally, another misconception about meditation is that it is a quick fix for all of life's problems. While meditation can provide numerous benefits for the mind and body, it is not a magic cure-all. Like any practice, it takes time and effort to see lasting results. Consistent practice is key in order to reap the full benefits of meditation.

Meditation is a practice that has numerous benefits for the mind and body, but it is important to understand what it is and what it is not. Meditation is not a religion, not a way to escape reality, and not a quick fix. By understanding these misconceptions, individuals can approach meditation with a more open and informed mindset.

Summary

Meditation is a powerful tool for improving mental and emotional well-being that has been practiced for thousands of years. It is a technique for training the mind and improving focus and awareness, and it is not inherently a religious practice or a way to escape reality. It is also important to note that meditation is not a quick fix, and consistent practice is necessary to see lasting results.

Despite these misconceptions, meditation has numerous proven benefits, including reducing stress and anxiety, improving sleep, increasing self-awareness, and enhancing overall well-being. With these benefits in mind, it is important to encourage everyone to try meditation and incorporate it into their daily routine.

In today's fast-paced and stressful world, taking time to slow down and connect with oneself is more important than ever. Meditation offers a simple and accessible way to do just that. By making meditation a consistent part of our routines, we can enhance our mental and emotional health, reduce stress and anxiety, and live happier and more satisfying lives.

Part II: IMPORTANCE OF MEDITATION

Benefits of Meditation

Meditation is a technique that has been practiced for thousands of years and has been known to have numerous benefits for both the mind and body. It involves focusing the mind on a particular object, thought, or activity to achieve a state of calm and relaxation. The following are some of the benefits of meditation:

Physical Benefits:

1. Improved immune system: Meditation has been shown to increase the activity of natural killer cells, which are responsible for fighting off viruses and cancer cells. A stronger immune system means fewer illnesses and a better overall health.

2. Reduced blood pressure: High blood pressure is a common health concern that can lead to heart disease and stroke. Meditation has been found to lower blood pressure by reducing stress and promoting relaxation.

3. Improved sleep quality: Meditation has been shown to improve the quality of sleep by reducing stress and promoting relaxation. People who meditate regularly report better sleep patterns and feel more refreshed upon waking up.

Mental Benefits:

1. Reduced stress and anxiety: Meditation is known to be an effective tool for reducing stress and anxiety. It has been found to lower the levels of the stress hormone cortisol, leading to a calmer and more relaxed state of mind.

2. Increased focus and concentration: Meditation requires focused attention on a particular object or activity, which helps to improve concentration and focus. People who meditate regularly report feeling more alert and focused throughout the day.

3. Improved emotional well-being: Meditation has been found to improve emotional well-being by reducing symptoms of depression and anxiety. It can also help to foster a more positive outlook on life and improve overall feelings of happiness and well-being.

The benefits of meditation cannot be overstated. It has been shown to improve both physical and mental health, making it a valuable tool for anyone looking to improve their overall well-being. Incorporating meditation into your daily routine can help you to achieve a greater sense of calm, focus, and balance in your life.

How to Meditate

Meditation is a simple yet powerful technique that can help you to achieve a state of calm and relaxation, reduce stress and anxiety, and improve your overall well-being. Here are some steps on how to meditate:

1. Finding a comfortable and quiet space: Choose a quiet and comfortable space where you won't be interrupted. You can sit on a cushion, a chair, or lie down. Make sure that your body is relaxed and comfortable.

2. Choosing a meditation technique: There are many different meditation techniques, so choose one that resonates with you. Some popular techniques include mindfulness meditation, guided meditation, and mantra meditation.

3. Breathing exercises: Focus on your breath as you meditate. Take slow, deep breaths, inhaling through your nose and exhaling through your mouth. You can count your breaths or focus on the sensation of the breath moving in and out of your body.

4. Setting a regular practice schedule: Set aside time each day to meditate. Even just a few minutes of meditation each day can have a positive impact on your well-being. Choose a time that works for you, whether it's first thing in the morning, during your lunch break, or before bed.

As you begin to meditate, it's important to remember that it's a practice, and it takes time to develop. Be patient with yourself, and don't worry if your mind wanders or you find it difficult to focus at first. With regular practice, you'll find it easier to achieve a state of calm and relaxation, and you'll reap the benefits of meditation in your daily life.

Incorporating Meditation into Daily Life

Incorporating meditation into your daily life can be a great way to reduce stress and anxiety, improve your focus and concentration, and increase your overall well-being. Here are some tips on how to make meditation a part of your daily routine:

1. Setting realistic goals: When starting a meditation practice, it's important to set realistic goals. Don't try to meditate for long periods of time right away, start with just a few minutes a day and gradually increase your practice time.

2. Starting small and gradually increasing practice time: Starting with just a few minutes of meditation each day can be a great way to build a consistent meditation practice. Over time, you can gradually increase your practice time to 10, 15, or even 20 minutes a day.

3. Finding a meditation community: Joining a meditation community can be a great way to stay motivated and committed to your practice. There are many online communities and local meditation groups that you can join to connect with others who share your interest in meditation.

4. Staying motivated and committing to the practice: It can be challenging to stay motivated and committed to a daily meditation

14

practice, especially when life gets busy. One way to stay motivated is to set aside a specific time each day for your practice and make it a non-negotiable part of your routine. You can also try different meditation techniques and mix up your practice to keep it interesting and engaging.

Incorporating meditation into your daily life can be a powerful tool for improving your well-being and reducing stress. By setting realistic goals, starting small and gradually increasing your practice time, finding a meditation community, and staying motivated and committed to the practice, you can make meditation a regular part of your daily routine.

Summary

Meditation is a practice that involves training the mind to focus and achieve a state of calmness and relaxation. It has been shown to have numerous benefits for our physical, mental, and emotional well-being.

Incorporating meditation into our daily lives can be a simple yet powerful way to reduce stress, improve our focus and concentration, and increase our overall sense of well-being. By setting realistic goals, starting small, finding a community, and staying motivated, we can make meditation a regular part of our daily routine.

I strongly encourage everyone to give meditation a try and experience the benefits for themselves. With practice and commitment, it's possible to experience a greater sense of peace, clarity, and contentment in our lives.

In a world that can be busy, stressful, and overwhelming, meditation can be a powerful tool to help us find balance and inner peace. So, take a deep breath, close your eyes, and give it a try. You may be surprised at the positive impact it can have on your life.

BENEFITS OF MEDITATION

Physical Benefits of Meditation

Meditation is a practice that has been shown to have numerous benefits for the human body. Many of these benefits are physical, and can help to improve overall health and well-being. In this section, we will explore some of the physical benefits of meditation.

One of the most common physical benefits of meditation is improved sleep quality. Meditation has been shown to help people fall asleep faster, stay asleep longer, and wake up feeling more refreshed. This is because meditation can help to reduce stress and anxiety, which are common causes of sleep problems.

Another physical benefit of meditation is that it can help to reduce blood pressure. High blood pressure is a major risk factor for heart disease and stroke, and reducing it can help to improve overall cardiovascular health. Meditation has been shown to be effective in reducing blood pressure in people who have hypertension.

Meditation has also been shown to boost the immune system. This is because meditation can help to reduce stress, which is a major contributor to a weakened immune system. By reducing stress, meditation can help to improve the body's ability to fight off infections and diseases.

Finally, meditation has been shown to be effective in reducing chronic pain. Chronic pain is a common problem that can be difficult to treat, but meditation can help to reduce pain by reducing stress and anxiety. This can help to improve overall quality of life for people who suffer from chronic pain.

Overall, the physical benefits of meditation are numerous and can help to improve overall health and well-being. By improving sleep quality, reducing blood pressure, boosting the immune system, and reducing chronic pain, meditation can help to improve the physical health of those who practice it.

Mental Benefits of Meditation

Meditation is not only beneficial for the physical body but also for the mind. It is a powerful tool for enhancing mental well-being and has been shown to have numerous benefits for the brain. In this section, we will explore some of the mental benefits of meditation.

One of the most well-known mental benefits of meditation is its ability to reduce stress and anxiety. Meditation can help to calm the mind and reduce the negative effects of stress on the body. It has also been shown to reduce symptoms of anxiety disorders and improve overall mental health.

Meditation has also been shown to enhance focus and concentration. This is because meditation involves training the mind to focus on a particular object or thought, which can help to improve the ability to concentrate on tasks. Regular meditation practice has been shown to improve cognitive abilities such as attention and memory.

Another mental benefit of meditation is that it can increase emotional stability. Meditation can help to regulate emotions and reduce the negative effects of emotional stressors. It has also been shown to improve mood and increase feelings of happiness and well-being.

Finally, meditation has been shown to improve memory retention. This is because meditation can help to improve the functioning of the brain's memory centers. Regular meditation practice has been shown to improve both short-term and long-term memory, as well as improve the ability to recall information.

Overall, the mental benefits of meditation are numerous and can help to improve overall mental health and well-being. By reducing stress and anxiety, enhancing focus and concentration, increasing emotional stability, and improving memory retention, meditation can help to improve the mental health of those who practice it.

Emotional Benefits of Meditation

Meditation has been known to provide emotional benefits in addition to physical and mental benefits. It can help people become more aware of their emotions, improve their ability to cope with stress, and increase their overall happiness and well-being. In this section, we will explore some of the emotional benefits of meditation.

Meditation can help individuals become more aware of their thoughts and emotions. By practicing mindfulness, individuals can observe their thoughts and feelings without judgment, which can help them identify negative patterns and behaviors. This increased self-awareness can lead to greater emotional intelligence, which can improve relationships and overall emotional health.

Meditation has been shown to improve empathy and compassion for oneself and others. By practicing loving-kindness meditation, individuals can cultivate feelings of kindness and compassion towards themselves and others. This can lead to more positive relationships and a greater sense of connection with others.

Meditation can also help reduce negative emotions such as anger, fear, and sadness. By practicing mindfulness, individuals can observe their negative emotions without judgment and learn to let them go. This can lead to greater emotional stability and a more positive outlook on life.

Finally, meditation has been shown to boost overall happiness and well-being. By reducing stress, improving self-awareness, and cultivating positive emotions, individuals who practice meditation report feeling happier and more content with their lives. This can lead to a greater sense of purpose and fulfillment.

The emotional benefits of meditation are numerous and can significantly improve one's overall well-being. By increasing self-awareness, improving empathy and compassion, reducing negative emotions, and boosting overall happiness, meditation can help individuals lead more fulfilling and emotionally healthy lives.

Spiritual Benefits of Meditation

Meditation has long been used as a tool for spiritual growth and enlightenment. While it has many physical and mental benefits, it also has significant spiritual benefits. In this section, we will explore some of the spiritual benefits of meditation.

Meditation can help individuals feel a greater sense of connection to the universe or a higher power. By practicing mindfulness and being present in the moment, individuals can become more aware of the interconnectedness of all things. This can lead to a greater sense of purpose and meaning in life.

Meditation has been shown to enhance intuition and creativity. By quieting the mind and focusing on the present moment, individuals can tap into their inner wisdom and creativity. This can lead to greater insight and clarity in decision-making and problem-solving.

Meditation can also deepen an individual's understanding of self and others. By practicing mindfulness and self-reflection, individuals can become more aware of their own thoughts, emotions, and behaviors. This can lead to greater self-awareness and empathy for others.

Finally, meditation can cultivate a sense of inner peace and calmness. By practicing mindfulness and being present in the moment, individuals can let go of stress, anxiety, and negative thoughts. This can lead to a greater sense of inner peace and calmness, even in the midst of difficult circumstances.

The spiritual benefits of meditation are numerous and can significantly enhance one's spiritual growth and enlightenment. By increasing a sense of connection to the universe, enhancing intuition and creativity, deepening understanding of self and others, and cultivating inner peace and calmness, meditation can help individuals lead a more spiritually fulfilling life.

Summary

Meditation is a powerful tool that can bring numerous benefits to our lives. We have explored the spiritual benefits of meditation, including an increased sense of connection to the universe, enhanced intuition and creativity, a deeper understanding of self and others, and a sense of inner peace and calmness.

With all of these benefits, it's no wonder that meditation has been used for centuries as a way to cultivate spiritual growth and enlightenment. Whether you are new to meditation or have been practicing for years, there is always something to gain from taking a few minutes each day to be present and focus on your breath.

Therefore, I encourage everyone to practice meditation regularly and to make it a part of your daily routine. The journey of spiritual growth and enlightenment can be long and challenging, but meditation can help make that journey a little easier and more fulfilling.

In the end, the importance of meditation lies in its ability to help us connect with our true selves and with the universe. It can help us find meaning and purpose in our lives, and it can bring us a sense of peace and calmness that is essential for our well-being. So, let's all take a few minutes each day to meditate and enjoy the many benefits that come with it.

Part II: What is Meditation?

<u>CHAPTER 4:</u>
DIFFERENT TYPES OF MEDITATION

Mindfulness Meditation

Mindfulness meditation is a form of meditation that originated from Buddhist teachings. It is a practice that involves being fully present in the moment, without judgment or distraction, and being aware of our thoughts, feelings, and sensations. Mindfulness meditation is often used as a tool to manage stress, anxiety, and depression, but it is also known to have many other benefits.

One of the main benefits of mindfulness meditation is that it helps to reduce stress and anxiety levels. When we practice mindfulness meditation, we learn to observe our thoughts and emotions without getting caught up in them, which can help to reduce feelings of overwhelm and anxiety. In addition, mindfulness meditation can help to increase feelings of happiness and well-being, improve memory and attention, and even reduce symptoms of chronic pain.

There are several techniques that can be used to practice mindfulness meditation. One of the most common techniques is to focus on the breath. This involves sitting in a comfortable position, closing your eyes, and bringing your attention to your breath. As you breathe in and out, you simply observe the sensation of the breath moving in and out of your body, without trying to control it in any way.

Another technique that can be used is body scan meditation. This involves lying down in a comfortable position and bringing your attention to different parts of your body, one at a time. As you focus on each body part, you observe any sensations you may be feeling, without judgment or distraction.

Finally, walking meditation is another technique that can be used to practice mindfulness. This involves taking a slow and deliberate walk, focusing on the sensations of your feet touching the ground, the movement of your body, and the sights and sounds around you.

Mindfulness meditation is a powerful tool that can help to reduce stress, anxiety, and depression, while also improving overall well-being. By practicing mindfulness meditation regularly, we can learn to be more present in the moment, and to appreciate the beauty of life around us.

Transcendental Meditation

Transcendental Meditation (TM) is a form of meditation that involves the use of a mantra – a sound, word, or phrase – to help the practitioner focus their mind and enter a state of deep relaxation. TM is often used as a tool for stress reduction, but it is also known to have many other benefits.

One of the main benefits of TM is that it can help to reduce stress and anxiety levels. When we practice TM, we enter a state of deep relaxation that allows our body to release tension and stress. In addition, TM has been shown to improve overall well-being, increase creativity and productivity, and even reduce symptoms of depression and anxiety.

The technique of TM involves sitting in a comfortable position with your eyes closed and repeating a mantra silently to yourself. The mantra is chosen by a certified TM teacher, based on the individual's personal characteristics and needs. The mantra is used as a tool to help the practitioner focus their mind and enter a state of deep relaxation.

During TM, the practitioner experiences a state of restful alertness, where their mind is fully awake and aware, but their body is deeply relaxed. This state is said to promote deep healing and rejuvenation within the body, as well as increased mental clarity and focus.

To practice TM, it is recommended to find a certified TM teacher who can provide personalized instruction and support. The teacher will guide the practitioner through the process of selecting a mantra and provide instruction on how to use the mantra to enter a state of deep relaxation. TM is typically practiced twice a day for 20 minutes each session.

Transcendental Meditation is a powerful tool that can help to reduce stress, anxiety, and improve overall well-being. By practicing TM regularly, we can learn to enter a state of deep relaxation and increase our mental clarity and focus. If you are interested in learning more about TM, it is recommended to find a certified TM teacher who can provide personalized instruction and support.

Loving-Kindness Meditation

Loving-kindness meditation, also known as Metta meditation, is a practice that cultivates feelings of kindness, compassion, and goodwill towards oneself and others. This form of meditation is rooted in Buddhist tradition and is believed to promote emotional and mental well-being.

The practice of loving-kindness meditation involves focusing on positive emotions and sending them out to oneself, loved ones, acquaintances, and even strangers. The goal is to cultivate feelings of love, kindness, and compassion towards oneself and others.

One of the main benefits of loving-kindness meditation is that it can help to reduce negative emotions such as anger, resentment, and anxiety. By focusing on positive emotions and sending them out to others, practitioners of loving-kindness meditation can experience a sense of calmness and inner peace.

In addition, loving-kindness meditation can improve relationships with others by promoting empathy and compassion. It can also increase feelings of gratitude and positivity, which can lead to a more optimistic outlook on life.

To practice loving-kindness meditation, it is recommended to find a quiet and comfortable place to sit or lie down. Begin by focusing on your breath and allowing your mind to settle. Then, start by sending feelings of love and kindness to yourself. You can repeat a series of phrases such as "may I be happy, may I be healthy, may I be safe, may I be at peace."

Once you have sent loving-kindness to yourself, you can move on to loved ones, acquaintances, and even strangers. You can repeat phrases such as "may they be happy, may they be healthy, may they be safe, may they be at peace." The goal is to cultivate feelings of love and kindness towards all living beings.

Loving-kindness meditation is a powerful tool that can promote emotional and mental well-being. By focusing on positive emotions and sending them out to oneself and others, practitioners of loving-kindness meditation can experience a sense of calmness, inner peace, and improved relationships with others. If you are interested in learning more about loving-kindness meditation, there are many resources available online and in-person classes that can provide instruction and support.

Yoga Meditation

Yoga meditation is a practice that combines physical movement, breath control, and mindfulness to promote a sense of relaxation, inner peace, and spiritual connection. It is an ancient practice that originated in India and has gained popularity all over the world as a form of exercise and stress relief.

The practice of yoga meditation involves performing poses, or asanas, while focusing on the breath and clearing the mind of distractions. This practice helps to cultivate a sense of mindfulness and can lead to greater awareness of the body, mind, and spirit.

One of the main benefits of yoga meditation is that it can help to reduce stress and anxiety. The physical movement and breath control help to calm the nervous system, while the mindfulness component helps to alleviate negative thoughts and emotions.

In addition, yoga meditation can improve overall physical health by increasing flexibility, strength, and balance. It can also improve mental health by promoting a sense of relaxation and reducing symptoms of depression and anxiety.

To practice yoga meditation, it is recommended to find a quiet and comfortable place to practice. Begin by focusing on the breath and allowing the mind to settle. Then, perform a series of poses, moving slowly and intentionally while focusing on the breath.

As you move through the poses, continue to focus on the breath and allow the mind to clear of distractions. You can repeat a mantra or visualization to help focus the mind and promote relaxation.

Yoga meditation is a powerful practice that can promote physical and mental well-being. By combining physical movement, breath control, and mindfulness, practitioners of yoga meditation can experience a sense of relaxation, inner peace, and spiritual connection. If you are interested in learning more about yoga meditation, there are many resources available online and in-person classes that can provide instruction and support.

Chakra Meditation

Chakra meditation is a practice that focuses on the seven energy centers, or chakras, in the body. Each chakra is associated with a different aspect of physical, emotional, and spiritual well-being, and the practice of chakra meditation aims to balance and align these energy centers for improved health and vitality.

The seven chakras are located along the spine, from the base to the crown of the head, and each is associated with a specific color, sound, and element. The first chakra, located at the base of the spine, is associated with the color red and the element of earth, while the seventh, located at the crown of the head, is associated with the color purple and the element of spirit.

The benefits of chakra meditation include improved physical, emotional, and spiritual health. By balancing and aligning the chakras, practitioners of chakra meditation may experience increased energy, reduced stress and anxiety, improved immune function, and greater spiritual awareness and connection.

To practice chakra meditation, it is recommended to find a quiet and comfortable place to practice. Begin by focusing on the breath and allowing the mind to settle. Then, focus on each chakra in turn, starting at the base of the spine and working your way up to the crown of the head.

As you focus on each chakra, visualize the associated color and element, and repeat a mantra or affirmation that corresponds to that chakra. You can also use physical movements, such as yoga poses or mudras, to stimulate and balance each chakra.

Chakra meditation is a powerful practice that can promote physical, emotional, and spiritual well-being. By balancing and aligning the seven energy centers in the body, practitioners of chakra meditation can experience increased energy, reduced stress and anxiety, improved immune function, and greater spiritual awareness and connection. If you are interested in learning more about chakra meditation, there are many resources available online and in-person classes that can provide instruction and support.

Summary

There are many different types of meditation, each with their own unique benefits and techniques. Mindfulness meditation is great for beginners who want to learn how to calm the mind and focus on the present moment. Loving-kindness meditation is perfect for those who want to cultivate compassion and kindness towards themselves and others. Transcendental meditation is a more structured practice that involves repeating a mantra to reach a state of deep relaxation and inner peace.

It can be overwhelming to choose which type of meditation to try, but it is important to remember that there is no right or wrong way to meditate. The key is to find a practice that resonates with you and that you enjoy. Trying different types of meditation can help you find what works best for you and your unique needs.

The benefits of meditation are numerous and can improve your mental, emotional, and physical health. By incorporating a regular meditation practice into your daily routine, you can experience reduced stress and anxiety, improved sleep, increased focus and concentration, and a greater sense of well-being.

Meditation is a powerful tool that can help you do just that. So, whether you are a beginner or an experienced meditator, I encourage you to continue exploring different types of meditation and discovering the many benefits that this practice has to offer.

CHAPTER 5:
WHAT MEDITATION IS NOT

Meditation is a practice that has gained significant popularity in recent years, with more and more people turning to meditation as a way to reduce stress, improve focus, and enhance overall well-being. However, it is important to understand what meditation is not, as this can help individuals approach the practice with the right mindset and expectations.

Firstly, meditation is not a religion. While meditation is often associated with certain spiritual practices, such as Buddhism or Hinduism, it does not require any specific religious beliefs or affiliations. In fact, meditation can be practiced by people of any religion, or even by those who do not follow a specific religious tradition.

Secondly, meditation is not a way to escape reality. While it can certainly help individuals relax and find a sense of calm, meditation is not about checking out of life or avoiding problems. Rather, it is about learning to be present in the moment, and accepting one's thoughts and feelings without judgment. This can help individuals develop a greater sense of self-awareness and emotional resilience, which can in turn help them face challenges in a more effective way.

Thirdly, meditation is not a quick fix. While some people may experience immediate benefits from meditation, such as feeling more relaxed or focused, it is important to understand that meditation is a practice that requires dedication and patience. Like any skill, it takes time to develop, and individuals who are committed to a regular meditation practice are more likely to experience long-term benefits.

Fourthly, meditation is not the only solution to mental health issues. While meditation can be a powerful tool for improving mental health, it is not a substitute for professional treatment. Individuals who are struggling with serious mental health issues should seek the help of a qualified mental health professional.

Finally, meditation is not limited to sitting still. While sitting meditation is perhaps the most well-known form of meditation, there are many other types of meditation practices, including movement-based practices like yoga and tai chi. It is important to explore different types of meditation to find what works best for each individual.

Understanding what meditation is not is just as important as understanding what it is. By approaching meditation with the right mindset and expectations, individuals can develop a more effective and sustainable meditation practice, and reap the many benefits that meditation has to offer.

Meditation is Not a Religion

Meditation is a practice that has been around for thousands of years and has been associated with various spiritual and religious traditions, such as Buddhism and Hinduism. However, it is important to note that meditation is not a religion in itself and can be practiced by people of any religion or no religion at all.

One of the benefits of meditation is that it is a non-denominational practice, meaning that it does not require any specific religious beliefs or affiliations. This makes it accessible to people from all walks of life, regardless of their cultural background, beliefs, or values. In fact, many people who practice meditation find that it enhances their spiritual practice, regardless of their religious affiliation.

For example, Christians can practice meditation as a way to deepen their relationship with God and connect with their inner selves. Muslims can practice meditation as a way to focus their minds and cultivate inner peace, which is an essential part of their faith. Similarly, Jews, Hindus, Buddhists, and people of other faiths can also incorporate meditation into their spiritual practices.

Moreover, there are many non-religious meditation practices that are accessible to people of all backgrounds. Some of these practices include mindfulness meditation, which involves focusing on the present moment and cultivating awareness of one's thoughts and feelings without judgment. Another non-religious meditation practice is transcendental meditation, which involves repeating a mantra or sound to achieve a deep state of relaxation and inner peace.

Other non-religious meditation practices include movement-based practices, such as yoga and tai chi, which combine physical movement with breath awareness and meditation techniques. These practices can help individuals reduce stress, improve flexibility and balance, and enhance overall well-being.

Meditation is not a religion and can be practiced by people of any religion or no religion at all. By incorporating meditation into their daily lives, individuals can cultivate inner peace, reduce stress, and enhance their overall well-being, regardless of their cultural background or beliefs.

Meditation is Not a Way to Escape Reality

Meditation is often misunderstood as a way to escape reality or avoid facing one's problems. However, in reality, meditation is a powerful tool that can help individuals face their problems head-on and cultivate inner strength and resilience. Meditation encourages individuals to be present in the moment and accept reality as it is, rather than trying to escape it.

Through regular meditation practice, individuals can learn to observe their thoughts and emotions without judgment, and develop a more compassionate and accepting attitude towards themselves and others. This can help individuals develop the necessary skills to face their problems with clarity, courage, and wisdom.

Furthermore, meditation can help individuals develop greater awareness and understanding of their own inner workings, including their thoughts, emotions, and behaviors. This self-awareness can help individuals identify patterns and habits that may be contributing to their problems, and develop new ways of thinking and behaving that can help them overcome their challenges.

Importantly, meditation also emphasizes the importance of being present in the moment, rather than dwelling on the past or worrying about the future. By focusing on the present moment, individuals can develop greater clarity and focus, and develop the necessary skills to cope with whatever challenges they may be facing.

Meditation is not a way to escape reality but rather a way to face reality with greater strength and resilience. Through regular meditation practice, individuals can learn to observe their thoughts and emotions without judgment, develop greater self-awareness and understanding, and cultivate the necessary skills to face their problems with clarity, courage, and wisdom. By being present in the moment, individuals can develop greater clarity and focus, and learn to cope with whatever challenges they may be facing.

Meditation is Not a Quick Fix

Meditation is often marketed as a quick fix for a variety of problems, such as stress, anxiety, and depression. However, in reality, meditation is not a quick fix and requires practice and dedication to see long-term benefits. Meditation is a skill that must be developed over time, and individuals must commit to a regular meditation practice to experience its full benefits.

One of the key reasons why meditation requires practice is that it involves training the mind to focus and concentrate. Just as a muscle becomes stronger with regular exercise, the brain also becomes more focused and attentive with regular meditation practice. Over time, individuals can learn to observe their thoughts and emotions without judgment, and develop greater self-awareness and understanding of their own inner workings.

Furthermore, meditation requires dedication and commitment to a regular practice. To see significant improvements in mental health and well-being, individuals must commit to a regular meditation practice, ideally on a daily basis. This means setting aside time each day to meditate, and making it a priority in one's daily routine.

Importantly, committing to a regular meditation practice can also help individuals develop greater discipline and self-control in other areas of their lives. By practicing mindfulness and self-awareness on a regular basis, individuals can become more attuned to their own needs and goals, and develop greater clarity and focus in their daily lives.

Meditation is not a quick fix but rather a skill that requires practice and dedication to see long-term benefits. By committing to a regular meditation practice, individuals can develop greater self-awareness, focus, and discipline, and experience significant improvements in their mental health and well-being.

Meditation is Not the Only Solution to Mental Health Issues

While meditation can be a powerful tool for improving mental health and well-being, it is not the only solution to mental health issues. In some cases, individuals may require additional treatments or support to address their mental health concerns. It is essential to understand how meditation can be used in conjunction with other treatments and to seek professional help when needed.

Firstly, meditation can be used in combination with other treatments, such as therapy or medication, to improve mental health outcomes. For example, mindfulness-based cognitive therapy (MBCT) is a treatment approach that combines mindfulness meditation with cognitive-behavioral therapy to treat conditions such as depression and anxiety. Similarly, some individuals may find that medication or other treatments help to alleviate symptoms of mental health conditions, while incorporating a regular meditation practice can further enhance their mental well-being.

It is important to note that meditation should not be used as a substitute for professional mental health treatment when needed. For individuals with severe or persistent mental health conditions, seeking professional help from a qualified mental health professional is essential. Meditation can be a valuable tool for improving mental health, but it is not a replacement for medication, therapy, or other treatments.

Furthermore, meditation may not be suitable for everyone. Some individuals may find that meditation exacerbates their symptoms or triggers feelings of discomfort or distress. It is important to approach meditation with a non-judgmental and compassionate attitude, and to seek guidance from a qualified meditation teacher if needed.

While meditation can be a powerful tool for improving mental health and well-being, it is not the only solution to mental health issues. It is important to understand how meditation can be used in conjunction with other treatments and to seek professional help when needed. By taking a holistic approach to mental health, individuals can develop a range of strategies and tools to support their mental well-being and thrive.

Meditation is Not Limited to Sitting Still

While many people associate meditation with sitting still in silence, there are actually a variety of movement-based meditation practices that exist. These practices can be just as effective in promoting mental clarity, relaxation, and overall well-being. In this article, we will explore some examples of movement-based meditation practices and how they can benefit individuals.

Firstly, movement-based meditation practices involve using physical movements as a way to focus the mind and cultivate inner awareness. These practices often involve a combination of movement, breathwork, and mindfulness techniques. By engaging the body and the mind, individuals can experience a sense of calm, clarity, and connection.

One example of a movement-based meditation practice is yoga. Yoga involves a series of physical postures, breathwork, and meditation techniques that can help to reduce stress, improve flexibility, and promote overall physical and mental well-being. Many people find that the combination of movement and mindfulness in yoga helps to quiet the mind and improve focus.

Another example of a movement-based meditation practice is Tai Chi. Tai Chi is a traditional Chinese martial art that involves a series of slow, flowing movements that are synchronized with deep breathing. Tai Chi has been shown to reduce stress, improve balance and coordination, and promote overall well-being.

Dance meditation is another example of a movement-based meditation practice. Dance meditation involves free-form movement and expression as a way to connect with the body and cultivate inner awareness. By allowing the body to move freely without judgment, individuals can release tension, reduce stress, and improve overall mood.

While sitting still meditation is one form of meditation practice, there are a variety of movement-based meditation practices that exist. These practices can be just as effective in promoting mental clarity, relaxation, and overall well-being. By exploring different styles of meditation, individuals can find a practice that resonates with them and supports their mental and physical health.

Summary

It is important to understand that meditation is not limited to sitting still in silence. While this is one form of meditation practice, there are a variety of movement-based meditation practices that can be just as effective in promoting mental clarity, relaxation, and overall well-being.

Understanding what meditation is not can help individuals to broaden their horizons and explore different styles of meditation that may resonate with them. It can also help to dispel misconceptions and myths around meditation, making it more accessible to a wider range of people.

Whether it is through sitting still, movement-based practices, or a combination of both, the benefits of meditation are undeniable. It can help to reduce stress, improve focus, promote relaxation, and enhance overall well-being. Therefore, it is important to continue exploring and practicing meditation, finding a practice that works best for each individual. With patience, persistence, and an open mind, anyone can experience the transformative power of meditation.

CHAPTER 6:
HOW TO MEDITATE

Importance of Learning how to Meditate

Meditation is an ancient practice that has been used for thousands of years to promote physical, mental, and emotional well-being. While it has its roots in spiritual and religious traditions, meditation is now widely recognized as a powerful tool for reducing stress, improving focus and concentration, and enhancing overall health and wellness. As such, there are many compelling reasons why it is important to learn how to meditate.

First and foremost, meditation is a highly effective way to manage stress. In today's fast-paced world, stress is a pervasive and often debilitating factor that can have serious negative consequences for our health and well-being. Meditation has been shown to reduce the levels of stress hormones in the body, thereby promoting greater relaxation, calmness, and emotional balance. Regular meditation practice can help to improve our ability to cope with stress, enabling us to lead happier and healthier lives.

In addition to reducing stress, meditation has been shown to improve focus and concentration. By cultivating a calm and clear mind, we are able to be more productive and efficient in our daily lives. Meditation has also been shown to enhance creativity, boost memory, and improve cognitive function, making it an ideal practice for anyone looking to sharpen their mental skills.

Meditation is also a powerful tool for improving physical health. Research has shown that regular meditation practice can help to lower blood pressure, reduce inflammation, and boost the immune system. It has also been shown to improve cardiovascular health, reduce the risk of chronic diseases, and promote overall vitality and well-being.

Beyond its physical and mental health benefits, meditation is a practice that can help us to develop greater self-awareness and self-understanding. By tuning in to our innermost thoughts and feelings, we can gain a deeper appreciation for who we are and what we value in life. This can lead to greater happiness, fulfillment, and a sense of purpose.

Learning how to meditate is an important step towards achieving greater health, happiness, and well-being. Whether you are looking to reduce stress, improve focus and concentration, or enhance your physical and mental health, meditation is a practice that can help you to achieve your goals. With regular practice and dedication, you can unlock the many benefits of meditation and live a more fulfilling and meaningful life.

Preparing for Meditation

Meditation is a practice that requires focus, concentration, and relaxation. To prepare for meditation, there are several key steps that you can take to create a conducive environment and mindset for your practice.

1. Find a quiet and comfortable space: The first step in preparing for meditation is to find a quiet and comfortable space where you can sit or lie down without being disturbed. This could be a separate room in your home, a quiet park or garden, or even a quiet corner of your workplace. It is important that the space is free from distractions and interruptions.

2. Eliminate distractions: Once you have found your quiet space, it is important to eliminate any distractions that could interfere with your meditation practice. This may include turning off your phone, closing the door, or using noise-cancelling headphones to block out external sounds.

3. Choose a time to meditate: It is important to choose a time to meditate that works for you and your schedule. This could be early in the morning before work, during your lunch break, or in the evening before bed. It is important to choose a time when you are least likely to be interrupted or distracted.

4. Get into a comfortable position: Whether you choose to sit or lie down, it is important to get into a comfortable position that allows you to relax and focus. This could be sitting cross-legged on a cushion or chair, or lying down on your back with your arms by your side. It is important to find a position that feels natural and comfortable for you.

5. Set an intention for your meditation practice: Before you begin your meditation practice, it is important to set an intention for what you hope to achieve from your practice. This could be to reduce stress, improve focus, or cultivate a sense of inner peace and calm. Setting an intention can help to focus your mind and give your meditation practice greater meaning and purpose.

Preparing for meditation is an important step in creating a conducive environment for your practice. By finding a quiet and comfortable space, eliminating distractions, choosing a time to meditate, getting into a comfortable position, and setting an intention for your practice, you can create the ideal conditions for a successful meditation practice.

Basic Meditation Techniques

Meditation is a practice that has been used for centuries to promote inner peace, relaxation, and mindfulness. There are several basic meditation techniques that can be practiced to help quiet the mind and reduce stress.

1. Focus on your breath: One of the simplest and most popular meditation techniques is to focus on your breath. Sit comfortably with your eyes closed and take a few deep breaths. Then, focus your attention on the sensation of your breath as it enters and leaves your body. If your mind wanders, gently bring your attention back to your breath.

2. Body scan meditation: Body scan meditation involves focusing your attention on different parts of your body, starting from your toes and moving up to your head. This technique can help to increase body awareness and promote relaxation.

3. Mantra meditation: Mantra meditation involves repeating a word or phrase, such as "Om" or "peace," in your mind. This technique can help to focus the mind and promote relaxation.

4. Visualization meditation: Visualization meditation involves creating a mental image of a peaceful place or situation, such as a beach or a garden. This technique can help to promote relaxation and reduce stress.

5. Loving-kindness meditation: Loving-kindness meditation involves focusing your attention on feelings of compassion and kindness towards yourself and others. This technique can help to cultivate positive emotions and promote inner peace.

There are several basic meditation techniques that can be practiced to promote relaxation, mindfulness, and inner peace. By focusing on your breath, practicing body scan meditation, repeating a mantra, visualizing a peaceful situation, or cultivating feelings of kindness and compassion, you can quiet your mind and reduce stress.

Tips for Maintaining Focus During Meditation

Maintaining focus during meditation can be challenging, especially for beginners. However, there are a few tips that can help you stay focused and get the most out of your meditation practice.

1. Acknowledge distractions: It's normal for your mind to wander during meditation. When you notice your thoughts drifting away, acknowledge the distraction and gently bring your attention back to your breath or chosen object of meditation.

2. Let go of thoughts: Don't become frustrated or discouraged by thoughts that arise during meditation. Instead, simply observe them without judgment and let them go. Try to return your focus to your breath or object of meditation.

3. Refocus on your breath or chosen object of meditation: If you find that your mind continues to wander, refocus your attention on your breath or chosen object of meditation. Use your breath as a anchor to bring your mind back to the present moment.

4. Be patient with yourself: Meditation is a practice that takes time and patience. Rather than getting frustrated with yourself when you find it difficult to stay focused, approach it with a gentle and compassionate attitude. Accept that your mind will wander, and continue to practice regularly.

Maintaining focus during meditation is not always easy, but it can be achieved with practice and patience. By acknowledging distractions, letting go of thoughts, refocusing on your breath or chosen object of meditation, and being patient with yourself, you can develop a more focused and mindful approach to your meditation practice.

Ending Your Meditation

Ending your meditation is just as important as starting it. It's a time to reflect on your practice and set intentions for the rest of your day. Here are a few tips on how to end your meditation practice:

1. Take a few deep breaths: Take a few deep breaths to ground yourself and bring your attention back to your body. Inhale deeply, filling your lungs with air, and exhale slowly, releasing any tension or stress.

2. Reflect on your meditation practice: Spend a few moments reflecting on your meditation practice. Notice any changes in your body or mind, and any new insights or realizations that came up during your practice. Reflecting on your practice can help you cultivate a deeper understanding of yourself and your meditation practice.

3. Set an intention for the rest of your day: Setting an intention for the rest of your day can help you stay mindful and focused as you move through your daily activities. Choose an intention that resonates with you, such as "I will approach each task with mindfulness and presence" or "I will cultivate gratitude and appreciation for the small things in life."

4. Slowly come back to your surroundings: Take your time as you come out of your meditation practice. Slowly open your eyes and take a few deep breaths before getting up. Take a moment to notice your surroundings and the sensations in your body before you move on with the rest of your day.

Ending your meditation practice is an important part of the process. By taking a few deep breaths, reflecting on your practice, setting an intention for the rest of your day, and slowly coming back to your surroundings, you can cultivate a more mindful and intentional approach to your daily life.

Summary

Regular meditation practice has numerous benefits for both the mind and body. From reducing stress and anxiety to improving focus and concentration, meditation can help us lead more balanced and fulfilling lives. By taking the time to explore different techniques and finding what works best for us, we can reap the rewards of a regular meditation practice.

I encourage you to continue exploring different meditation techniques and finding what resonates with you. Whether it's a guided meditation, mindfulness practice, or a mantra meditation, there are countless ways to incorporate meditation into your daily routine.

Remember, meditation doesn't have to be complicated or time-consuming. Simply finding a quiet space, focusing on your breath, and being present in the moment can be a powerful meditation practice. By making meditation a regular part of your life, you can experience the numerous benefits that come with a more mindful and intentional approach to living.

So, take a deep breath, find a comfortable position, and begin your meditation practice. May you find peace, clarity, and a deeper connection to yourself and the world around you through your meditation practice.

Part III: Benefits of Meditation

<u>CHAPTER 6:</u>

THE PHYSICAL BENEFITS OF MEDITATION

Meditation, a practice that has been around for thousands of years, is gaining popularity in the modern world as a way to improve physical and mental health. Meditation involves focusing one's attention, often on the breath, to achieve a state of relaxed awareness. It is known to have a variety of benefits, including reducing stress, improving mental clarity, and promoting emotional stability. However, in this chapter, we will focus specifically on the physical benefits of meditation. Physical health is crucial for overall well-being, and meditation has been shown to improve various aspects of physical health. The purpose of this outline is to explore the physical benefits of meditation in detail, explaining how meditation affects the body and highlighting the importance of including meditation in a healthy lifestyle.

Body Benefits

Meditation has been shown to have a variety of positive effects on the body, including lowering blood pressure. Blood pressure is the force that blood exerts on the walls of the blood vessels as it flows through them. High blood pressure, or hypertension, is a common condition that can lead to serious health problems such as heart disease, stroke, and kidney failure.

Meditation has been found to lower blood pressure in several ways. One way is by reducing the body's production of stress hormones such as cortisol and adrenaline. These hormones can cause blood vessels to constrict, leading to higher blood pressure. By reducing their production, meditation can help to relax the blood vessels and lower blood pressure.

Another way that meditation can lower blood pressure is by improving the functioning of the nervous system. The nervous system is responsible for regulating blood pressure, and when it is overactive, it can contribute to hypertension. Meditation has been shown to activate the parasympathetic nervous system, which helps to reduce stress and lower blood pressure.

The benefits of lowered blood pressure are numerous. Lower blood pressure reduces the strain on the heart and blood vessels, which can reduce the risk of heart disease and stroke. It also improves the functioning of the kidneys and can reduce the risk of kidney failure. Additionally, lower blood pressure can improve overall quality of life by reducing symptoms such as headaches, dizziness, and fatigue.

Meditation is a powerful tool for improving physical health, and one of its many benefits is the ability to lower blood pressure. By reducing stress hormones and activating the parasympathetic nervous system, meditation can help to relax the blood vessels and improve the functioning of the cardiovascular system. The benefits of lowered blood pressure include a reduced risk of heart disease, stroke, and kidney failure, as well as improved overall quality of life.

Improved Breathing

Breathing is an essential function of the human body. It is the process of inhaling oxygen and exhaling carbon dioxide, which is necessary for survival. However, many people do not breathe properly, which can lead to a variety of health problems. Meditation has been found to improve breathing in several ways, leading to numerous benefits for overall health and well-being.

One of the primary ways that meditation improves breathing is by increasing awareness of the breath. Many people breathe shallowly or hold their breath without realizing it, which can contribute to stress and anxiety. Through meditation, individuals learn to focus on their breath, noticing the sensations of inhaling and exhaling. This increased awareness can help individuals to breathe more deeply and fully, improving oxygen intake and reducing stress.

Another way that meditation improves breathing is by reducing stress and anxiety. Stress and anxiety can cause individuals to breathe more rapidly and shallowly, which can lead to hyperventilation and other breathing problems. By reducing stress and anxiety levels, meditation can help individuals to breathe more calmly and deeply, promoting relaxation and reducing the risk of breathing-related health problems.

The benefits of improved breathing are numerous. Deep breathing can improve oxygen intake and reduce the risk of respiratory problems such as asthma and bronchitis. It can also reduce stress and anxiety, leading to improved mental health and well-being. Additionally, deep breathing can improve digestion, reduce muscle tension, and promote better sleep.

Meditation is a powerful tool for improving breathing and overall health. By increasing awareness of the breath and reducing stress and anxiety, meditation can help individuals to breathe more deeply and fully, promoting relaxation and reducing the risk of breathing-related health problems. The benefits of improved breathing include better oxygen intake, reduced risk of respiratory problems, improved mental health and well-being, improved digestion, reduced muscle tension, and better sleep.

Reduced Inflammation

Inflammation is a natural response of the body's immune system to protect against infections, injuries, or other harmful stimuli. However, chronic inflammation can lead to numerous health problems, including heart disease, cancer, and autoimmune diseases. Meditation has been found to reduce inflammation, leading to numerous benefits for overall health and well-being.

One of the primary ways that meditation reduces inflammation is by reducing stress. Stress triggers the release of cortisol, a hormone that can contribute to inflammation. By reducing stress levels, meditation can help to decrease cortisol levels, which in turn, reduces inflammation. Studies have shown that individuals who practice meditation regularly have lower levels of inflammatory markers in their blood.

Another way that meditation reduces inflammation is by activating the parasympathetic nervous system. The parasympathetic nervous system is responsible for the body's "rest and digest" response, which promotes relaxation and reduces inflammation. Meditation can activate the parasympathetic nervous system, leading to reduced inflammation and improved overall health.

The benefits of reduced inflammation are numerous. Chronic inflammation can lead to numerous health problems, including heart disease, cancer, and autoimmune diseases. By reducing inflammation, meditation can help to reduce the risk of these diseases and improve overall health. Additionally, reduced inflammation can improve mental health and well-being, leading to reduced stress and anxiety levels.

Meditation is a powerful tool for reducing inflammation and improving overall health. By reducing stress levels and activating the parasympathetic nervous system, meditation can help to decrease inflammation and reduce the risk of numerous health problems. The benefits of reduced inflammation include improved overall health, reduced risk of chronic diseases, and improved mental health and well-being.

Enhanced Immune System

The immune system is the body's natural defense against infections and diseases. It is a complex system that consists of various cells, tissues, and organs that work together to protect the body from harmful pathogens. Meditation has been found to enhance the immune system, leading to numerous benefits for overall health and well-being.

One of the primary ways that meditation enhances the immune system is by reducing stress. Stress can weaken the immune system, making it more difficult for the body to fight off infections and diseases. By reducing stress levels, meditation can help to strengthen the immune system, leading to improved overall health and well-being.

Another way that meditation enhances the immune system is by increasing the activity of natural killer cells. Natural killer cells are a type of immune cell that play a critical role in fighting off infections and diseases. Studies have shown that individuals who practice meditation regularly have higher levels of natural killer cell activity, leading to improved immune function.

Additionally, meditation has been found to increase the production of antibodies, which are proteins that help the body to fight off infections. By increasing the production of antibodies, meditation can help to improve the body's ability to fight off infections and diseases.

The benefits of an enhanced immune system are numerous. A strong immune system can help to prevent infections and diseases, leading to improved overall health and well-being. Additionally, an enhanced immune system can improve the body's response to vaccines, leading to improved protection against infectious diseases.

Meditation is a powerful tool for enhancing the immune system and improving overall health and well-being. By reducing stress levels, increasing natural killer cell activity, and increasing the production of antibodies, meditation can help to strengthen the immune system and improve the body's ability to fight off infections and diseases. The benefits of an enhanced immune system include improved overall health, reduced risk of infections and diseases, and improved response to vaccines.

Reduced Chronic Pain

Chronic pain is a persistent and often debilitating condition that affects millions of people worldwide. It is defined as pain that lasts for more than three months and can be caused by a variety of factors, including injury, disease, and psychological factors. Meditation has been found to be an effective tool for reducing chronic pain, leading to numerous benefits for those who suffer from this condition.

One of the primary ways that meditation reduces chronic pain is by reducing stress levels. Stress can exacerbate chronic pain, making it more difficult to manage. By reducing stress levels, meditation can help to alleviate the symptoms of chronic pain and improve overall well-being.

Additionally, meditation can help to increase the production of endorphins, which are natural painkillers produced by the body. By increasing the production of endorphins, meditation can help to alleviate the symptoms of chronic pain and improve overall comfort.

Moreover, meditation can help to improve the brain's ability to process pain. Chronic pain can cause changes in the brain that make it more difficult to process pain signals. By practicing meditation regularly, individuals can help to rewire their brains and improve the brain's ability to process pain, leading to reduced symptoms of chronic pain.

The benefits of reduced chronic pain are numerous. Individuals who suffer from chronic pain often experience a significant reduction in their quality of life. By reducing chronic pain, meditation can help to improve overall well-being and lead to a more fulfilling life. Additionally, reducing chronic pain can help to improve mood, reduce anxiety and depression, and improve sleep quality.

Meditation is a powerful tool for reducing chronic pain and improving overall well-being. By reducing stress levels, increasing the production of endorphins, and improving the brain's ability to process pain, meditation can help to alleviate the symptoms of chronic pain and improve quality of life. The benefits of reduced chronic pain include improved overall well-being, reduced anxiety and depression, and improved sleep quality.

Summary

Meditation is a practice that offers numerous physical benefits to those who practice it regularly. From reducing stress and anxiety to improving sleep quality and reducing chronic pain, meditation has been found to be an effective tool for improving overall well-being. By increasing self-awareness, mindfulness, and compassion, meditation can help individuals achieve a greater sense of balance and harmony in their lives.

If you have yet to try meditation, I encourage you to give it a try. Whether you are looking to reduce stress, improve your physical health, or simply become more present and mindful in your daily life, meditation can offer a wide range of benefits. It is a simple and accessible practice that can be done anywhere, at any time.

CHAPTER 7:
EMOTIONAL BENEFITS OF MEDITATION

Meditation is a practice that has been used for thousands of years to cultivate inner peace, reduce stress, and promote overall well-being. At its core, meditation involves training the mind to focus and become more aware of the present moment.

There are many different types of meditation, each with their own unique techniques and benefits. However, they all share a common goal: to help us connect with our inner selves and find greater clarity and calmness in our lives.

One of the most significant benefits of meditation is the emotional benefits it provides. Studies have shown that regular meditation can help reduce symptoms of anxiety, depression, and stress, and improve overall emotional well-being.

Through meditation, we learn to cultivate a sense of inner peace and balance, which can help us better manage our emotions and respond to challenging situations with greater clarity and calmness. It can also help us develop greater compassion and empathy towards ourselves and others, leading to deeper, more meaningful relationships.

In this chapter, we will explore the many emotional benefits of meditation and provide practical guidance on how to incorporate this powerful practice into your daily life. Whether you are a beginner or an experienced meditator, this book will help you develop a deeper understanding of meditation and how it can help you achieve greater emotional well-being.

Reduction of Stress and Anxiety

Stress and anxiety are common experiences in today's fast-paced world, and can have a negative impact on our physical and emotional health. Fortunately, meditation has been proven to be an effective tool for reducing stress and anxiety.

Meditation works by activating the body's natural relaxation response, which helps to reduce the levels of stress hormones such as cortisol and adrenaline. By quieting the mind and focusing on the present moment, we can break the cycle of negative thoughts and emotions that often contribute to feelings of stress and anxiety.

Research has shown that regular meditation can have a significant impact on reducing stress and anxiety. In one study, participants who practiced meditation for just eight weeks experienced a 51% reduction in symptoms of anxiety. Another study found that mindfulness meditation can help reduce symptoms of depression and anxiety, and improve overall emotional well-being.

Personal anecdotes from meditators also highlight the positive effects of meditation on stress and anxiety. Many people report feeling more relaxed and centered after practicing meditation, and have found it to be an effective tool for managing their emotions and improving their overall quality of life.

Increased Emotional Regulation

Emotional regulation is the ability to manage and control one's own emotions in response to different situations. It is an important skill that can impact our personal and professional lives. Meditation has been shown to be a powerful tool for increasing emotional regulation.

Meditation helps with emotional regulation by improving our ability to focus and become more aware of our thoughts and emotions. Through meditation, we learn to observe our thoughts and emotions without judgment, which allows us to better understand and manage them.

Research has shown that meditation can have a significant impact on emotional regulation. In one study, participants who practiced meditation for just eight weeks showed increased activity in the prefrontal cortex, which is responsible for regulating emotions. Another study found that mindfulness meditation can help regulate emotions in individuals with mood disorders such as depression and anxiety.

Personal anecdotes from meditators also highlight the positive effects of meditation on emotional regulation. Many people report feeling more in control of their emotions and better able to manage stress and difficult situations after practicing meditation. Some have even found that meditation has helped them break free from negative thought patterns and improve their overall quality of life.

Improved Self-Awareness and Empathy

Improved self-awareness and empathy are two important benefits of meditation. By practicing meditation regularly, we can become more aware of our thoughts and emotions, and develop a greater understanding and compassion for others.

Meditation improves self-awareness by helping us focus on the present moment and become more attuned to our physical and emotional sensations. This increased awareness can help us identify and manage our emotions more effectively, which can lead to better decision-making and a greater sense of inner peace.

In terms of empathy, meditation can help us develop a greater understanding and compassion for others by cultivating a sense of connection and shared humanity. Through meditation, we learn to be more present and attentive in our interactions with others, and to approach them with openness and kindness.

Research has shown that meditation can have a significant impact on self-awareness and empathy. In one study, participants who practiced mindfulness meditation for just two weeks showed increased activity in brain regions associated with self-awareness and empathy. Another study found that meditation can improve empathy and reduce bias towards others who are perceived as different.

Personal anecdotes from meditators also highlight the positive effects of meditation on self-awareness and empathy. Many people report feeling more connected to themselves and others, and more able to respond with compassion and understanding in challenging situations. Some have even found that meditation has helped them develop a greater sense of purpose and meaning in their lives.

Improved Mood and Emotional Well-Being

Improved mood and emotional well-being are two significant benefits of meditation. By practicing meditation regularly, we can learn to manage our emotions more effectively and develop a greater sense of inner peace and happiness.

Meditation improves mood and emotional well-being by helping us cultivate a more positive and accepting attitude towards our thoughts and emotions. Through meditation, we learn to observe our thoughts and feelings without judgment, which can help us develop a greater sense of calm and balance.

In terms of emotional well-being, meditation can help us develop greater resilience and coping skills, which can help us manage stress, anxiety, and other negative emotions more effectively. Through meditation, we can learn to quiet our minds and cultivate a greater sense of inner peace, which can help us feel more grounded and centered.

Research has shown that meditation can have a significant impact on mood and emotional well-being. In one study, participants who practiced mindfulness meditation for just eight weeks reported significant improvements in their overall sense of well-being, including reduced feelings of anxiety and depression.

Another study found that meditation can help reduce symptoms of post-traumatic stress disorder (PTSD) and improve overall emotional well-being in veterans. Other studies have found that meditation can help reduce symptoms of anxiety and depression in individuals with chronic pain or other medical conditions.

Personal anecdotes from meditators also highlight the positive effects of meditation on mood and emotional well-being. Many people report feeling more calm, centered, and emotionally balanced after practicing meditation, and some have even found that meditation has helped them manage chronic pain or other medical conditions more effectively.

Summary

Meditation is a powerful tool for improving mood and emotional well-being. By practicing meditation regularly, we can learn to observe our thoughts and emotions without judgment and develop greater resilience and coping skills. Research has shown that meditation can have a significant impact on reducing symptoms of anxiety, depression, and PTSD, as well as improving overall emotional well-being.

If you have never tried meditation before, now is the perfect time to start. There are many resources available online, including guided meditations and apps that can help you get started. Remember that meditation is a practice, and it may take time to develop the habit and see the full benefits. But with patience and persistence, you can cultivate a greater sense of inner peace and emotional balance.

By prioritizing self-care and incorporating meditation into our daily routine, we can improve our overall quality of life and experience greater happiness and fulfillment. So, take a deep breath, close your eyes, and give meditation a try. Your mind and body will thank you.

CHAPTER 8:
MENTAL BENEFITS

Mental health is a crucial aspect of our overall well-being. It affects how we feel, think, and behave, influencing our daily lives in a significant way. Given the fast-paced lifestyle and work pressures that we face today, maintaining mental health has become increasingly challenging. This is where meditation comes in as an effective way to promote mental wellness. Meditation is a practice that involves training the mind to focus and achieve a state of calmness and relaxation. It has become a popular tool for improving mental health, with numerous studies showing its benefits in reducing stress, anxiety, depression, and enhancing overall well-being. This essay will focus on the mental benefits of meditation, highlighting its importance in promoting mental health.

Reduced Anxiety and Stress

Anxiety and stress are two common mental health issues that affect millions of people worldwide. Anxiety is a feeling of unease or worry, often accompanied by physical symptoms such as increased heart rate, sweating, and difficulty sleeping. Stress, on the other hand, is a response to external pressures, such as work or personal responsibilities, that can lead to physical and emotional exhaustion. Both anxiety and stress can have a significant impact on a person's mental and physical health, leading to a range of negative outcomes if left untreated.

Research has shown that meditation can be an effective tool for reducing anxiety and stress. A study published in the Journal of Psychosomatic Research found that mindfulness meditation reduced symptoms of anxiety and depression in patients with generalized anxiety disorder. Another study published in the Journal of Behavioral Medicine found that practicing meditation for just 10 minutes a day reduced symptoms of stress and improved overall well-being.

Meditation works to reduce anxiety and stress by promoting relaxation and mindfulness. During meditation, the body's relaxation response is triggered, which reduces the activity of the sympathetic nervous system, responsible for the "fight or flight" response. This, in turn, leads to a reduction in heart rate, blood pressure, and muscle tension, creating a sense of calmness and relaxation in the body. Additionally, meditation helps to cultivate mindfulness, which involves paying attention to the present moment without judgment. This can help individuals develop a more positive and accepting attitude towards their thoughts and feelings, reducing anxiety and stress levels over time.

The practice of meditation can have a significant impact on reducing anxiety and stress, promoting mental wellness and overall well-being. By reducing the activity of the sympathetic nervous system and cultivating mindfulness, individuals can experience a greater sense of calmness and relaxation, leading to improved mental health outcomes.

Improved Mood

Mood disorders are a category of mental health conditions that affect a person's emotional state and can lead to significant impairment in daily functioning. Examples of mood disorders include depression, bipolar disorder, and seasonal affective disorder (SAD). These conditions can cause a range of symptoms, including persistent sadness, loss of interest in activities, changes in appetite, and difficulty sleeping.

Research has shown that meditation can be an effective tool for improving mood disorders. A study published in the Journal of Affective Disorders found that mindfulness-based cognitive therapy (MBCT) reduced symptoms of depression in patients with a history of recurrent depression. Another study published in the Journal of

Psychiatric Practice found that regular meditation practice improved symptoms of anxiety and depression in patients with bipolar disorder.

Meditation works to improve mood by promoting changes in brain activity and increasing feelings of well-being. During meditation, the brain experiences increased activity in the prefrontal cortex, which is responsible for regulating emotions and controlling impulsive behavior. This can help individuals better regulate their emotions and reduce symptoms of depression and anxiety. Additionally, meditation helps to cultivate positive emotions such as compassion, gratitude, and joy, leading to an overall improvement in mood.

Overall, the practice of meditation can have a significant impact on improving mood disorders. By promoting changes in brain activity and cultivating positive emotions, individuals can experience greater feelings of well-being and reduced symptoms of depression and anxiety.

Increased Self-Awareness

Self-awareness is the ability to recognize and understand one's thoughts, emotions, and behaviors. It involves being in tune with one's inner experiences, as well as how those experiences are perceived by others. Developing self-awareness can lead to greater personal growth, improved relationships, and better decision-making.

Research has shown that meditation can be an effective tool for increasing self-awareness. A study published in the journal *Consciousness and Cognition* found that mindfulness meditation improved self-awareness and attentional control. Another study published in the *Journal of Personality and Social Psychology* found that meditation led to greater self-awareness and increased self-esteem.

Meditation increases self-awareness by helping individuals become more present and focused on their inner experiences. During meditation, individuals are encouraged to observe their thoughts and emotions without judgment, which can lead to a greater understanding of their inner workings. Additionally, meditation can help individuals identify patterns of thought and behavior that may be holding them back, allowing them to make positive changes and live more authentic lives.

Through regular meditation practice, individuals can develop a deeper understanding of themselves and their inner experiences. By cultivating greater self-awareness, individuals can improve their relationships, make better decisions, and live more fulfilling lives.

Enhanced Focus and Concentration

Focus and concentration are the abilities to direct one's attention to a specific task or object and maintain that attention over a sustained period of time. These skills are essential for achieving goals, completing tasks, and being productive.

Research has shown that meditation can be an effective tool for enhancing focus and concentration. A study published in the journal *Frontiers in Human Neuroscience* found that mindfulness meditation improved cognitive control and attentional performance. Another study published in the *Journal of Alternative and Complementary Medicine* found that meditation led to greater attentional focus and decreased mind wandering.

Meditation enhances focus and concentration by training the mind to stay present and focused on the task at hand. During meditation, individuals are encouraged to focus on their breath or a specific object, and to bring their attention back to that object whenever their mind wanders. This practice helps strengthen the neural pathways associated with attention and cognitive control, making it easier to focus and concentrate outside of meditation.

Additionally, meditation can help reduce distractions and improve mental clarity, allowing individuals to stay focused on their goals and tasks. By developing greater focus and concentration through meditation, individuals can improve their productivity, achieve their goals more efficiently, and experience a greater sense of calm and clarity throughout their day.

Meditation can be an effective tool for enhancing focus and concentration, and can lead to a more productive and fulfilling life.

Improved Sleep

Sleep disorders refer to a variety of conditions that affect the quality and quantity of sleep. These disorders can range from insomnia and sleep apnea to restless leg syndrome and narcolepsy. Sleep disorders can cause daytime fatigue, irritability, and difficulty concentrating, and can have a significant impact on overall health and well-being.

Research has shown that meditation can be an effective tool for improving sleep. A study published in the Journal of Clinical Sleep Medicine found that mindfulness meditation improved sleep quality and reduced symptoms of insomnia. Another study published in the journal Sleep Medicine found that meditation led to improvements in sleep duration, sleep efficiency, and overall sleep quality.

Meditation improves sleep by reducing stress and anxiety, which are common causes of sleep disorders. Meditation helps to calm the mind and body, reducing the physiological effects of stress and promoting relaxation. This can lead to a more peaceful and restful sleep.

Additionally, meditation can help individuals develop greater awareness and control over their thoughts and emotions. This can help them to identify and address any underlying issues that may be contributing to their sleep problems. By addressing these issues, individuals can reduce their stress levels and improve their overall quality of life.

Meditation can also promote a more consistent sleep schedule, which is important for maintaining healthy sleep patterns. By establishing a regular meditation practice, individuals can train their bodies to relax and prepare for sleep at the same time each day. This can help to regulate their sleep-wake cycle, leading to more restful and refreshing sleep.

Meditation can be an effective tool for improving sleep and addressing sleep disorders. By promoting relaxation, reducing stress and anxiety, and promoting a more consistent sleep schedule, meditation can help individuals achieve a more restful and rejuvenating sleep.

Summary

Meditation offers a wide range of mental benefits, including reduced stress and anxiety, improved focus and concentration, and increased feelings of happiness and well-being. By incorporating meditation into your daily routine, you can cultivate a greater sense of calm and balance in your life.

If you have not yet tried meditation, I encourage you to give it a try. There are many resources available, from guided meditations to meditation apps and classes, that can help you get started. Remember that meditation is a practice, and like any skill, it takes time and dedication to see results. Be patient with yourself and trust the process.

Finally, I believe that meditation is a powerful tool that can help us navigate the challenges of daily life with greater ease and resilience. By taking the time to cultivate a regular meditation practice, we can experience the many mental and emotional benefits that come with it. So why not give it a try? You may be surprised at how much it can enhance your life.

Part IV: Getting Started with Meditation

Meditation has become an increasingly popular practice in recent years due to its numerous benefits for mental and physical health. Having a dedicated meditation space can enhance the practice and create a more serene and peaceful environment. It can also serve as a reminder to prioritize self-care and make time for mindfulness. In this outline, we will explore the steps involved in setting up a meditation space and the benefits that come with having a designated area for meditation.

Choosing the Space

When selecting a space to meditate, there are certain factors that should be taken into consideration to ensure that the experience is as positive and beneficial as possible. These factors include privacy, quietness, lighting, and comfort.

Privacy is an important consideration when choosing a meditation space. It is important to find a space that is free from distractions and interruptions. This could be a separate room in your home, a corner of a room, or even an outdoor space that is private and secluded.

Quietness is also crucial for a successful meditation practice. The space should be free from external noise and distractions such as loud music, traffic, or other people's conversations. This will help you to focus your mind and achieve a deeper state of relaxation.

Lighting is another important factor to consider when selecting a meditation space. It is best to choose a space that has natural light, as this can help to create a calming and peaceful environment. However, if natural light is not available, soft and gentle lighting can also be used to create a relaxing atmosphere.

Comfort is the last but not least consideration when choosing a meditation space. The space should be comfortable and inviting, with a cushion or chair to sit on, and any other necessary accessories such as a mat or blanket. This will help to make the experience more enjoyable and help you to focus on your practice.

When choosing a meditation space, it is important to consider privacy, quietness, lighting, and comfort. By selecting a space that meets these criteria, you will be able to create an environment that is conducive to a successful and fulfilling meditation practice.

Clearing the Space

Clearing the space for meditation is an essential part of creating an environment that is conducive to relaxation and inner peace. There are several steps you can take to clear the space and create a more peaceful and calming atmosphere.

The first step in clearing the space for meditation is to remove any clutter. This could include items that are not related to your meditation practice, such as books, papers, or other objects. Removing clutter can help to create a more open, spacious feeling in the room, which can be beneficial for meditation.

The second step is to clean the area. This could include dusting, vacuuming, or wiping down surfaces. A clean and tidy space can help to create a more peaceful and relaxing environment, which can be essential for meditation.

The third step is to remove any distractions. This could include turning off your phone or other electronic devices, closing windows or doors to block out noise, and removing any other sources of distraction from the room. Removing distractions can help you to focus your mind and achieve a deeper state of relaxation during your meditation practice.

Clearing the space for meditation is an important part of creating an environment that is conducive to relaxation and inner peace. By removing clutter, cleaning the area, and removing distractions, you can create a space that is more conducive to meditation and help to support your practice.

Setting up the Space

Setting up the space for meditation is an important step in creating an environment that is conducive to relaxation and inner peace. There are several things you can do to personalize your meditation space and create a calm, peaceful atmosphere that supports your practice.

The first step in setting up the space for meditation is to select a meditation cushion or chair. This will help to provide you with a comfortable and supportive seating arrangement that will allow you to sit for extended periods of time. A cushion or chair will also help to maintain proper posture, which can be beneficial for your physical and mental well-being.

The second step is to add a personal touch to the space. This could include decorations such as artwork, photos, or other items that inspire you. You could also add incense or candles to create a calming aroma that can help to promote relaxation and concentration. Plants or flowers can also be a great addition to your space, as they can help to create a more natural and calming atmosphere.

When it comes to decorations, it's important to choose items that resonate with you and bring you joy. This could be anything from a favorite piece of artwork to a sentimental object that holds special meaning. Adding these personal touches can help to create a more meaningful and inspiring meditation space.

Incense or candles can also be a great addition to your meditation space. The aroma of incense or the flickering flame of a candle can help to create a calming and soothing atmosphere that can promote relaxation and concentration.

Finally, adding plants or flowers to your space can help to create a more natural and calming environment. Plants can help to purify the air and create a sense of vitality, while flowers can add color and beauty to your space.

Setting up the space for meditation is an important part of creating an environment that supports your practice. By selecting a comfortable seating arrangement, adding personal touches, and incorporating calming elements such as incense or plants, you can create a space that is soothing, inspiring, and conducive to inner peace.

Creating a Ritual

Creating a ritual for meditation is an important step in establishing a consistent and effective meditation practice. By developing a pre-meditation routine and incorporating mindfulness practices, you can create a meaningful and effective ritual that supports your meditation practice.

The first step in creating a ritual for meditation is to develop a pre-meditation routine. This could include activities such as stretching, taking a few deep breaths, or practicing relaxation techniques. By taking these steps before beginning your meditation practice, you can help to calm your mind and prepare your body for the practice ahead.

Incorporating mindfulness practices into your ritual can also be beneficial. This could include deep breathing exercises, which can help to calm the mind and body, and promote relaxation. By focusing on your breath, you can help to quiet your thoughts and become more present in the moment.

Another mindfulness practice that can be incorporated into your meditation ritual is a body scan. This involves focusing on each part of your body, from your toes to the top of your head, and noticing any sensations or areas of tension. By bringing your awareness to your body in this way, you can help to release tension and promote relaxation.

In addition to these mindfulness practices, you may also want to incorporate other elements into your meditation ritual that are meaningful to you. This could include lighting candles or incense, playing calming music, or reciting a mantra or affirmation.

Ultimately, the key to creating a meaningful and effective meditation ritual is to find practices that work for you and that you enjoy. By taking the time to develop a pre-meditation routine and incorporating mindfulness practices into your meditation practice, you can create a ritual that supports your overall well-being and helps you to cultivate a deeper sense of inner peace and calm.

Maintaining the Space

Maintaining the space for meditation is an important aspect of supporting a consistent and effective meditation practice. By keeping the space clean and making adjustments as needed, you can create an environment that supports relaxation, focus, and inner peace.

Regular cleaning and upkeep is a key component of maintaining the space for meditation. This could include dusting, vacuuming, and wiping down any surfaces in the room where you meditate. By keeping the space clean and free of clutter, you can create a more peaceful and calming environment.

In addition to regular cleaning, it is important to make adjustments to the space as needed. This could include adding or removing furniture, changing the lighting, or adjusting the temperature in the room. By making these adjustments, you can create a space that feels comfortable and welcoming, and that supports your meditation practice.

Another important aspect of maintaining the space for meditation is creating a sense of sacredness and intentionality in the space. This could include adding meaningful decorations or symbols, such as candles, crystals, or images that inspire you. By infusing the space with your own personal energy and intention, you can create a more powerful and supportive environment for your meditation practice.

It is also important to create a routine for maintaining the space for meditation. This could include setting aside time each week to clean and tidy the space, or making a habit of lighting candles or incense before each meditation session. By establishing a routine, you can create a sense of consistency and ritual in your meditation practice, which can help to deepen your connection to the practice itself.

Maintaining the space for meditation is an ongoing process that requires attention and care. By keeping the space clean and making adjustments as needed, you can create an environment that supports relaxation, focus, and inner peace, and that helps you to cultivate a deeper sense of connection to yourself and to the practice of meditation.

Summary

Having a dedicated space for meditation can provide numerous benefits to our mental and physical well-being. By creating a peaceful and welcoming environment, we can deepen our meditation practice and cultivate a deeper sense of connection to ourselves.

A dedicated meditation space can help us to reduce stress, improve focus and concentration, and promote overall feelings of calm and relaxation. It can also serve as a reminder to prioritize self-care and mindfulness in our daily lives.

If you haven't already done so, we encourage you to set up a space for meditation in your own home. It doesn't have to be elaborate or expensive - even a small corner of a room can be transformed into a peaceful oasis with a few simple additions.

By taking the time to create a dedicated space for meditation, you are taking an important step towards prioritizing your mental and physical health. Whether you are a seasoned meditator or just starting out, having a designated space can help you to deepen your practice and cultivate a greater sense of inner peace and well-being.

CHAPTER 9:

CHOOSING A TIME TO MEDITATE

Meditation has become an increasingly popular practice for reducing stress, improving mental clarity, and enhancing overall well-being. However, many beginners overlook the importance of choosing a specific time to meditate. Having a consistent meditation schedule helps create a habit, improves focus and concentration, and can even lead to better sleep. In this article, we will explore the benefits of choosing a time to meditate and offer tips for finding the best time that works for your individual needs and lifestyle. Whether you're a morning person or a night owl, we hope to inspire you to incorporate meditation into your daily routine and reap the many benefits it has to offer.

Benefits of Choosing a Specific Time to Meditate

1. Consistency in practice:

Choosing a specific time to meditate helps create consistency in your practice. This means you are more likely to stick to your meditation routine, and you will be able to build upon your progress. When you meditate at the same time every day, your mind and body start to expect it, making it easier to get started and stay focused.

2. Creating a habit:

Meditating at the same time every day helps create a habit. Habits are powerful because they become automatic, and you don't have to rely on willpower or motivation to keep going. When you make meditation a habit, it becomes a natural part of your daily routine, and you're more likely to stick with it over the long term.

3. Improved focus and concentration:

When you meditate at the same time every day, it can improve your focus and concentration. By making meditation a regular part of your routine, you train your mind to focus and concentrate better during your practice. This can carry over into other areas of your life, such as work or school, where focus and concentration are critical.

4. Better sleep:

Meditating at the same time every day can lead to better sleep. Meditation helps reduce stress and relaxes the body, making it easier to fall asleep and stay asleep. When you meditate at the same time every day, your body starts to associate that time with relaxation, creating a natural cue for your mind and body to wind down and prepare for sleep.

Choosing a specific time to meditate has numerous benefits. It helps create consistency in your practice, creates a habit, improves focus and concentration, and can lead to better sleep. By finding a time that works for your individual needs and lifestyle, you can start reaping the benefits of a consistent meditation practice.

Factors to Consider When Choosing a Time to Meditate

When deciding on a time to meditate, there are several factors to consider to ensure that you can maintain a consistent practice. Here are some key factors to consider:

1. Personal schedule:

One of the most important factors to consider when choosing a time to meditate is your personal schedule. If you have a busy workday, you might find it difficult to meditate in the morning. On the other hand, if you have a more relaxed schedule in the morning, you may find it easier to fit in a meditation practice at that time.

2. Natural energy levels:

Another important factor to consider is your natural energy levels. Some people may naturally feel more alert and focused in the morning, while others may feel more energized in the afternoon or evening.

Consider your own natural energy patterns and choose a time when you can meditate at your most alert and focused state.

3. Time of day:

The time of day can also play a role in choosing a time to meditate. For example, many people find that meditating in the morning helps them set a positive tone for the rest of the day. Others may prefer to meditate in the evening to unwind and relax after a long day.

4. Daily routines:

Your daily routines can also impact the time you choose to meditate. If you have a regular morning routine, you may want to incorporate meditation into that routine. Alternatively, if you have a regular evening routine, you may find it easier to meditate at the end of the day.

When choosing a time to meditate, it's important to consider your personal schedule, natural energy levels, time of day, and daily routines. By taking these factors into account, you can choose a time that works best for you and establish a consistent meditation practice.

Morning Meditation

Morning meditation is a practice of starting your day with a few moments of stillness, mindfulness, and reflection. This practice has numerous benefits and can help you set a positive tone for the rest of your day. Here are some advantages of starting your day with meditation:

1. Reduces stress and anxiety:

Meditation is an effective tool for reducing stress and anxiety. By practicing morning meditation, you can start your day with a calm and clear mind, which can help you manage stress and anxiety throughout the day.

2. Increases focus and productivity:

Morning meditation can also help increase your focus and productivity. By taking a few moments to clear your mind and focus on your breath, you can improve your concentration and mental clarity, which can help you be more productive throughout the day.

3. Improves overall well-being:

Morning meditation can help you improve your overall well-being. It can help you connect with your inner self and develop a sense of inner peace, which can help you feel more centered and balanced throughout the day.

Here are some tips for making morning meditation a habit:

1. Set a regular time:

Choose a regular time for your morning meditation practice and stick to it. This will help you establish a routine and make it easier to make meditation a habit.

2. Start small:

If you're new to meditation, start with just a few minutes each day and gradually increase the length of your practice as you feel more comfortable.

3. Create a calming environment:

Create a calming environment for your morning meditation practice. Choose a quiet and clutter-free space, and consider lighting a candle or playing calming music to help you relax.

4. Be patient and persistent:

Remember that developing a meditation practice takes time and patience. Be persistent and keep practicing, even if you don't notice immediate results.

Starting your day with morning meditation can have numerous benefits for your mental, emotional, and physical well-being. By following these tips, you can make morning meditation a habit and reap the rewards of a consistent meditation practice.

Evening Meditation

Evening meditation is a practice of winding down and relaxing before bedtime. Just like morning meditation, this practice has numerous benefits and can help you end your day on a positive note. Here are some advantages of ending your day with meditation:

1. Reduces stress and anxiety:

Meditation is an effective tool for reducing stress and anxiety. By practicing evening meditation, you can release the tension and worries of the day, and cultivate a sense of calm and relaxation.

2. Improves sleep quality:

Evening meditation can also help improve your sleep quality. By calming your mind and body, you can prepare yourself for a restful night's sleep, and wake up feeling refreshed and rejuvenated.

3. Enhances self-awareness:

Evening meditation can help you reflect on your day and develop a greater sense of self-awareness. By observing your thoughts and emotions, you can gain insight into your habits and patterns, and make positive changes in your life.

Here are some tips for avoiding distractions during evening meditation:

1. Set a regular time:

Choose a regular time for your evening meditation practice and stick to it. This will help you establish a routine and make it easier to make meditation a habit.

2. Silence your phone:

Turn off your phone or put it in silent mode to avoid distractions during your meditation practice. You can also use a meditation app that provides guided meditations and timers to help you stay focused.

3. Create a calming environment:

Create a calming environment for your evening meditation practice. Dim the lights, light a candle, and play soothing music to help you relax and unwind.

4. Practice deep breathing:

Practice deep breathing exercises to help you calm your mind and body. Inhale deeply through your nose, hold for a few seconds, and exhale slowly through your mouth.

Ending your day with evening meditation can have numerous benefits for your mental, emotional, and physical well-being. By following these tips, you can avoid distractions and cultivate a sense of calm and relaxation, and prepare yourself for a restful night's sleep.

Mid-Day Meditation

Mid-day meditation is a practice of taking a break from your daily routine to relax and rejuvenate your mind and body. It has numerous benefits and can help you stay focused, reduce stress, and improve your overall well-being. Here are some advantages of taking a break for meditation during the day:

1. Improves productivity:

Mid-day meditation can improve your productivity by helping you stay focused and alert. By taking a break to meditate, you can recharge your energy and increase your mental clarity.

2. Reduces stress and anxiety:

Meditation is a proven tool for reducing stress and anxiety. By practicing mid-day meditation, you can release the tension and stress that may have built up during the day, and cultivate a sense of calm and relaxation.

3. Boosts creativity:

Mid-day meditation can also help boost your creativity. By calming your mind and body, you can tap into your inner creativity and generate new ideas.

Here are some tips for incorporating mid-day meditation into a busy schedule:

1. Schedule it:

Schedule your mid-day meditation practice in your calendar, just like any other important meeting or appointment. This will help you prioritize your meditation practice and make it a regular part of your daily routine.

2. Keep it short:

You don't need to meditate for hours to reap the benefits of mid-day meditation. Even a short 10-15 minute meditation practice can help you relax and recharge your energy.

3. Find a quiet place:

Find a quiet place where you can meditate without interruptions. This can be a quiet corner in your office, a nearby park, or even your car.

4. Use guided meditations:

If you find it hard to meditate on your own, use guided meditations to help you stay focused and calm. There are many meditation apps and websites that offer guided meditations for free.

Mid-day meditation is a powerful tool for staying focused, reducing stress, and improving your overall well-being. By following these tips, you can incorporate mid-day meditation into your busy schedule and enjoy the benefits of a regular meditation practice.

Flexibility in Choosing a Time to Meditate

Flexibility in choosing a time to meditate is an important aspect of maintaining a consistent meditation practice. Life can be unpredictable, and our schedules can change at a moment's notice. By being flexible with our meditation practice, we can adapt to these changes and ensure that we continue to prioritize our mental and emotional well-being. Here are some reasons why flexibility is important, and some tips for adapting to changes in schedule:

Importance of Being Flexible:

1. Maintains Consistency: Being flexible with your meditation practice allows you to maintain consistency, even when your schedule

changes. This consistency can help you to develop a regular meditation habit, which is key to experiencing the benefits of meditation.

2. Reduces Stress: If you have a rigid meditation schedule, you may feel stressed or anxious if you can't stick to it. Being flexible with your practice can help you to reduce stress and avoid feelings of guilt or frustration.

3. Increases Adaptability: Being flexible with your meditation practice can help you to become more adaptable in other areas of your life. This can help you to deal with unexpected events or changes in your routine more easily.

Tips for Adapting to Changes in Schedule:

1. Be Open to Change: The first step to being flexible with your meditation practice is to be open to change. Recognize that your schedule may change, and that it's okay to adjust your meditation practice accordingly.

2. Find Alternative Times: If you can't meditate at your usual time, try to find an alternative time that works for you. This could be early in the morning, during your lunch break, or in the evening.

3. Shorten Your Practice: If you don't have as much time as usual, try shortening your meditation practice. Even a few minutes of meditation can be beneficial.

4. Use Guided Meditations: If you're having trouble focusing, try using guided meditations. These can help you to stay on track and maintain your focus, even if your mind is busy.

5. Be Kind to Yourself: Remember, the most important thing is to be kind to yourself. Don't beat yourself up if you can't meditate at your usual time or for your usual length of time. Just do what you can, and know that any amount of meditation is better than none.

Being flexible with your meditation practice is an important aspect of maintaining a consistent meditation habit. By being open to change and adapting to your schedule, you can reduce stress, increase adaptability, and experience the benefits of meditation.

Summary

Choosing a time to meditate has numerous benefits that can positively impact our mental and emotional well-being. From reducing stress to increasing focus and adaptability, meditation can help us to live a more mindful and fulfilling life. It's important to be flexible and adaptable with our meditation practice, as life can be unpredictable and our schedules can change at any moment. By experimenting with different times and finding what works best for our personal practice, we can develop a consistent meditation habit and reap the rewards of this powerful practice. So, if you haven't already, take some time to explore different meditation times and find what works best for you. Your mind and body will thank you for it.

CHAPTER 10:
CHOOSING A MEDITATION TECHNIQUE

In today's fast-paced world, meditation has become an increasingly popular practice to relieve stress and improve overall well-being. It involves focusing the mind on a particular object or activity to achieve a state of calm and relaxation. However, with so many different types of meditation techniques available, it can be overwhelming to choose the one that is best for us. The importance of selecting the right meditation technique cannot be overstated, as it can greatly affect the quality of our meditation experience and the benefits we receive from it. This article will discuss the different types of meditation techniques and the factors to consider when choosing the appropriate one for our needs.

Understanding the Types of Meditation

Meditation is a practice that has been used for centuries to achieve a state of relaxation and inner peace. There are several types of meditation techniques, each with its own unique approach and benefits. Here are three of the most popular types:

1. Concentration meditation: This type of meditation involves focusing the mind on a single object, such as the breath or a mantra. The goal is to develop a deep concentration and focus, which can lead to improved cognitive function and reduced stress.

2. Mindfulness meditation: This technique involves being present in the moment and observing thoughts and feelings without judgment. It can help reduce stress and increase self-awareness, leading to better decision-making and improved emotional regulation.

3. Reflective meditation: This type of meditation involves contemplating a specific topic or question, such as the meaning of life or a personal problem. It can help with self-reflection, gaining insights, and finding solutions to problems.

When choosing a meditation technique, it's important to consider your goals and preferences. For example, if you want to reduce stress, mindfulness meditation may be the best choice. If you're looking for insights or solutions to a problem, reflective meditation may be more suitable. Ultimately, the key is to find a technique that resonates with you and that you can practice regularly to experience the benefits.

Factors to Consider in Choosing a Meditation Technique

Meditation is a powerful tool for improving mental and physical health. However, choosing the right meditation technique can be challenging, especially for beginners. Here are some key factors to consider when selecting a meditation technique:

1. Personal preferences: Meditation techniques vary widely in terms of their focus, style, and length. Some people prefer to focus on their breath, while others prefer guided meditations or visualization

techniques. It's important to choose a technique that resonates with your personal preferences and interests.

2. Physical abilities: Some meditation techniques require a certain level of physical ability, such as sitting cross-legged on the floor or maintaining a specific posture. If you have physical limitations, it's important to choose a technique that is comfortable and accessible for you.

3. Health conditions: Certain health conditions may require modifications to your meditation practice. For example, if you have chronic pain, you may need to use a chair or cushion to support your body during meditation. If you have a history of trauma or anxiety, you may want to choose a technique that is gentle and non-invasive.

4. Goals: Meditation can be used for a variety of purposes, such as reducing stress, improving focus, or promoting emotional wellbeing. It's important to choose a technique that aligns with your goals and intentions for meditation.

Ultimately, the key to choosing a meditation technique is to experiment and find what works best for you. Try different techniques and styles to find the one that resonates with your personal preferences, physical abilities, health conditions, and goals. With practice and patience, you can develop a regular meditation practice that supports your overall health and wellbeing.

Techniques for Concentration Meditation

Concentration meditation is a technique that involves focusing your attention on a single object or thought to improve your ability to concentrate. Here are three popular techniques for concentration meditation:

1. Breath Meditation: This technique involves focusing your attention on your breath. Sit comfortably with your back straight and your eyes closed. Take a few deep breaths, and then allow your breath

to settle into its natural rhythm. Focus your attention on the sensation of your breath as it enters and leaves your body. If your mind starts to wander, gently bring it back to your breath.

2. Mantra Meditation: In this technique, you repeat a word or phrase (known as a mantra) to help focus your mind. Choose a word or phrase that has personal meaning to you, such as "peace" or "love." Sit comfortably with your back straight and your eyes closed. Repeat your mantra silently to yourself, allowing your mind to focus on the sound and vibration of the word. If your mind starts to wander, gently bring it back to your mantra.

3. Object Meditation: This technique involves focusing your attention on a physical object, such as a candle or a flower. Sit comfortably with your back straight and your eyes open. Choose an object to focus on, and place it at eye level. Focus your attention on the object, observing its shape, color, and texture. If your mind starts to wander, gently bring it back to the object.

The key to concentration meditation is to choose a technique that resonates with you and to practice regularly. Start with just a few minutes of meditation each day and gradually increase the time as you become more comfortable. With practice and patience, you can improve your ability to concentrate and focus your mind.

Techniques for Mindfulness Meditation

Mindfulness meditation is a practice that involves paying attention to the present moment without judgment. Here are three popular techniques for mindfulness meditation:

1. Body Scan Meditation: This technique involves bringing awareness to different parts of your body, one at a time. Lie down or sit comfortably with your eyes closed. Start at the top of your head, and slowly scan down your body, paying attention to any sensations or feelings you notice. If you notice any tension or discomfort, simply

observe it without judgment and then move on to the next part of your body.

2. Walking Meditation: In this technique, you bring awareness to your body as you walk. Find a quiet place to walk, either indoors or outdoors. Start by standing still and taking a few deep breaths. Then, begin to walk slowly, paying attention to the sensation of your feet touching the ground, the movement of your legs, and the rhythm of your breath. If your mind starts to wander, gently bring it back to the sensation of walking.

3. Loving-Kindness Meditation: This technique involves cultivating feelings of love and compassion towards yourself and others. Sit comfortably with your eyes closed. Begin by bringing to mind someone you love, and silently repeat phrases of loving-kindness to them, such as "may you be happy and healthy." Then, bring to mind someone you feel neutral towards, and repeat the same phrases. Finally, bring to mind someone you have difficulty with, and repeat the phrases to them. Through this practice, you can cultivate feelings of love and compassion towards all beings.

The key to mindfulness meditation is to practice regularly and to be gentle with yourself when your mind wanders. Start with just a few minutes of meditation each day and gradually increase the time as you become more comfortable. With practice and patience, you can develop greater awareness and presence in your daily life.

Techniques for Reflective Meditation

Reflective meditation is a practice that involves looking inward and contemplating personal experiences and emotions. Here are three popular techniques for reflective meditation:

1. Visualization Meditation: This technique involves visualizing a scene or image in your mind's eye. Sit comfortably with your eyes closed and focus on your breath. Then, bring to mind a scene or image

that evokes a particular emotion or feeling. For example, you could visualize a peaceful beach or a beautiful sunset. Allow the scene to become vivid in your mind and notice any emotions or sensations that arise.

2. Contemplative Meditation: This technique involves contemplating a particular question or topic. Sit comfortably and focus on your breath. Then, bring to mind a question or topic that you would like to explore. For example, you could contemplate the meaning of happiness or the nature of suffering. Allow your mind to explore the question or topic, noticing any thoughts or insights that arise.

3. Inquiry Meditation: This technique involves questioning your own beliefs and assumptions. Sit comfortably and focus on your breath. Then, bring to mind a particular belief or assumption that you hold. For example, you could question the belief that success leads to happiness. Explore the belief or assumption, asking yourself questions such as "why do I believe this?" and "is this belief serving me?" Allow yourself to be open to new perspectives and insights.

The key to reflective meditation is to approach it with an open mind and a willingness to explore your own experiences and emotions. Start with just a few minutes of meditation each day and gradually increase the time as you become more comfortable. With practice and patience, you can develop greater insight and understanding of yourself and the world around you.

Finding the Appropriate Meditation Technique

Meditation is a personal practice, and not all techniques work for everyone. Finding the appropriate meditation technique can be challenging, but it's important to find the right one to reap its benefits. Here are some tips to find the appropriate meditation technique for you:

1. Try different techniques: There are many meditation techniques available, and each one has its own benefits. Experiment with different techniques to find the one that suits you best. For example, you can try mindfulness meditation, loving-kindness meditation, or body scan meditation. Do some research on the different techniques available and try a few to see which one resonates with you.

2. Take time to adjust: It takes time to adjust to a new meditation practice. Don't give up if you don't see immediate results. Give yourself a few weeks to adjust to the new technique and see if it works for you. If it doesn't, try a different technique.

3. Consult with a meditation teacher: A meditation teacher can help you find the appropriate technique for you. They can also help you with any challenges you might face during your meditation practice. A meditation teacher can provide guidance and support and help you deepen your practice.

Finding the appropriate meditation technique takes time and patience. Trying different techniques, taking time to adjust, and consulting with a meditation teacher can help you find the right technique for you. Remember, the most important thing is to find a technique that resonates with you and that you can practice consistently.

Summary

Choosing the appropriate meditation technique is essential for a successful and enriching meditation practice. Every individual is unique, and what works for one person may not work for another. Therefore, it is vital to explore and experiment with different meditation techniques until you find the one that resonates with you. Remember, finding the right meditation technique takes time, patience, and practice. Don't be discouraged if you don't see immediate results; keep exploring until you find the technique that works best for you. Choosing the appropriate meditation technique can help you reap the benefits of meditation, such as stress reduction, improved focus, and better mental and emotional well-being. So, take the time to find the right technique for you, and enjoy the journey of self-discovery and growth through meditation.

Part V: Common Obstacles and How to Overcome Them

Meditation is a practice that has been gaining popularity due to its numerous benefits for mental and physical health. However, many people find it challenging to meditate consistently due to various obstacles that arise during the practice. Common obstacles in meditation include restlessness and distractions, difficulty in focusing, and finding time to meditate. Understanding and overcoming these obstacles is important for a successful meditation practice. In this article, we will explore these obstacles in detail and provide tips on how to overcome them.

CHAPTER 11:
OBSTACLES MOST OFTEN FACED

Restlessness and Distractions

Restlessness and distractions are common obstacles that many people face when attempting to meditate. These obstacles can be frustrating and can make it difficult to maintain focus during the practice.

Causes of restlessness and distractions can vary, but they often stem from our busy minds and the endless stream of thoughts that can occupy our attention. Other external factors, such as noise or discomfort, can also contribute to restlessness and distractions during meditation.

To overcome restlessness and distractions during meditation, there are several tips that can be helpful:

1. Find a quiet and comfortable space: Choosing a quiet and comfortable space to meditate can help minimize external distractions

and make it easier to focus on the practice. This could be a designated meditation room or simply a quiet corner of your home.

2. Focus on your breath: One effective way to overcome distractions is to focus on your breath. Pay attention to the sensation of the breath as it enters and leaves your body. If your mind wanders, simply bring your attention back to your breath.

3. Acknowledge the distractions and let them go: It's natural for the mind to wander during meditation, and it's important to acknowledge those distractions without getting caught up in them. Simply observe them, acknowledge them, and then let them go.

4. Practice regularly: Regular meditation practice can help train the mind to stay focused and prevent restlessness and distractions. Start with short sessions and gradually increase the length of your practice as your focus improves.

Restlessness and distractions can be common obstacles when meditating. By understanding the causes and implementing these tips, you can overcome these obstacles and enjoy a more effective and fulfilling meditation practice.

Difficulty in Focusing

Difficulty in focusing is a common problem faced by people when they first start meditating. It can be frustrating when you are trying to still your mind, but your thoughts keep drifting away. This difficulty can be caused by a variety of factors, including stress, anxiety, and a busy mind.

To overcome the difficulty in focusing when meditating, there are several tips that can be helpful:

1. Start with short meditation sessions: If you are new to meditation, it can be helpful to start with short sessions. This can help you get used to the practice and gradually build up your focus over time.

2. Use guided meditations: Guided meditations can be helpful for those who struggle to focus. They provide a structure and guidance for your thoughts, which can help you stay focused and centered.

3. Use a mantra or visualization: Some people find it helpful to use a mantra or visualization to help them focus during meditation. This could be a word or phrase that you repeat to yourself, or a mental image that you visualize.

4. Experiment with different meditation techniques: Meditation techniques can vary widely, and what works for one person may not work for another. Experiment with different techniques to find what works best for you.

Difficulty in focusing when meditating is a common problem, but there are several tips that can help you overcome it. By starting with short sessions, using guided meditations, using a mantra or visualization, and experimenting with different techniques, you can gradually build up your focus and enjoy the benefits of a more effective meditation practice.

Finding Time to Meditate

Finding time to meditate can be a challenge in today's fast-paced world. With so many demands on our time, it can be difficult to set aside a few moments for ourselves to meditate. However, making time for meditation is essential for our mental and emotional well-being. In this article, we will discuss the causes of difficulty in finding time to meditate and tips to overcome this difficulty.

Causes of difficulty in finding time to meditate:

1. Busy schedules: Many of us have busy schedules, with work, family, and other responsibilities taking up much of our time.

2. Lack of prioritization: Sometimes, we may not prioritize meditation in our daily routine, and it can fall by the wayside.

3. Distractions: Social media, phone notifications, and other distractions can make it difficult to focus on meditation.

Tips to overcome difficulty in finding time to meditate:

1. Set a regular schedule for meditation: One of the best ways to find time to meditate is to set a regular schedule. This could be first thing in the morning, during your lunch break, or before bed. By making it a regular part of your routine, you are more likely to stick with it.

2. Find small pockets of time throughout the day: You don't need to have an hour to meditate. You can find small pockets of time throughout the day, such as waiting for a meeting to start or waiting in line at the grocery store. Use these moments to meditate for a few minutes.

3. Make meditation a priority: Make meditation a priority in your life. Recognize the value it brings to your mental and emotional well-being, and make it a non-negotiable part of your daily routine.

4. Reduce time spent on social media or other distractions: Social media and other distractions can be a major time-waster. By reducing the time spent on these activities, you can free up more time for meditation.

Finding time to meditate can be a challenge, but it is essential to our well-being. By setting a regular schedule, finding small pockets of time, making meditation a priority, and reducing distractions, we can carve out time for meditation in our busy lives.

Summary

There are common obstacles in meditation that can make it difficult to find time to practice. These obstacles include busy schedules, a lack of prioritization, and distractions. However, with some simple tips, it is possible to overcome these obstacles and continue practicing meditation regularly.

It is important to remember that the benefits of meditation are numerous. Regular meditation can help reduce stress and anxiety, improve focus and concentration, and promote overall mental and emotional well-being. By making meditation a priority and finding time to practice regularly, we can experience these benefits and improve our quality of life.

In summary, don't give up on meditation if you encounter obstacles. Instead, use the tips provided to overcome them and continue practicing. The rewards of regular meditation are well worth the effort, and you will soon find that it becomes an essential part of your daily routine.

Part VI: Tips for Making Meditation a Habit

Meditation is a practice that has been utilized for thousands of years to promote relaxation, reduce stress, and improve overall well-being. It involves focusing one's attention on a particular object, thought, or activity to achieve a state of mental clarity and calmness. Despite the numerous benefits of meditation, making it a regular habit can be a challenge for many people. With the constant distractions and demands of daily life, finding the time and motivation to meditate can be difficult. However, the benefits of meditation are too significant to ignore, making it essential to develop strategies to make meditation a part of our daily routine. In this outline, we will explore tips for making meditation a habit, including starting small, being consistent, and finding a meditation buddy.

CHAPTER 12:
MAINTAINING YOUR MEDITATION HABITS

Start Small

Starting small is an effective strategy for making meditation a habit. When we begin with small, manageable goals, it becomes easier to incorporate meditation into our daily routine. Starting small helps to reduce the pressure and expectations that can come with a new habit, making it more sustainable in the long run.

One way to start small with meditation is to begin by meditating for just a few minutes each day. This may sound like a minimal amount of time, but it can make a significant difference in a person's ability to establish a regular practice. Over time, as the habit becomes more automatic, we can gradually increase the amount of time spent meditating.

Another helpful tip is to incorporate meditation into an existing routine. For example, taking a few minutes to meditate before getting out of bed in the morning or before going to sleep at night can be an effective way to establish the habit. By linking meditation to an already established routine, it becomes easier to remember to meditate and to make it a regular part of our day.

Starting small with meditation also allows us to build confidence and momentum. As we begin to see the benefits of just a few minutes of meditation each day, we may feel more motivated to increase the amount of time we spend meditating. Over time, this can lead to a more significant and sustained meditation practice, with benefits that extend far beyond the actual time spent meditating.

Be Consistent

Being consistent with meditation is crucial for making it a habit. Consistency helps to establish a routine and makes it easier to maintain the practice over time. By committing to a regular meditation schedule, we can experience the full benefits of meditation and make it a sustainable part of our lives.

One way to be consistent with meditation is to meditate at the same time each day. This can help to create a habit and make it easier to remember to meditate. Whether it's first thing in the morning, during a lunch break, or before bed, finding a consistent time to meditate can help to establish a regular practice.

Another helpful tip for consistency is to start with a manageable amount of time. It's better to meditate for a few minutes each day and be consistent than to meditate for a longer period but only do it occasionally. By starting small and being consistent, we can gradually increase the amount of time spent meditating and build a sustainable habit.

Consistency also helps to create a sense of commitment to the practice. When we commit to meditating regularly, it becomes a priority in our lives, and we are more likely to make time for it. Over time, the habit of meditating regularly becomes automatic, and we may find ourselves naturally drawn to the practice.

In conclusion, being consistent with meditation is essential for making it a habit. By finding a consistent time to meditate, starting small, and committing to the practice, we can build a sustainable habit that can have a transformative impact on our lives.

Find A Meditation Buddy

Finding a meditation buddy can be a helpful tool in establishing a consistent meditation practice. Having someone to meditate with can provide accountability, motivation, and support, making it easier to make meditation a habit.

Finding a meditation buddy can be as simple as asking a friend or family member if they would like to meditate with you. Alternatively, joining a meditation group can be a great way to meet like-minded individuals and find a meditation partner. Many meditation groups offer guided meditations, workshops, and retreats, providing an opportunity to deepen your practice and connect with others.

Having a meditation buddy can provide a sense of accountability to your practice. Knowing that someone else is depending on you to show up can be a powerful motivator to meditate regularly. Additionally, having someone to discuss your meditation practice with can help you to stay motivated and engaged with the practice.

A meditation buddy can also provide encouragement and support. Meditating with someone else can help to create a sense of community and shared experience. By meditating together, you can celebrate each other's successes and provide support during challenging times.

Finding a meditation buddy can be an effective way to establish a consistent meditation practice. By joining a meditation group or asking a friend to meditate with you, you can find support, accountability, and motivation to make meditation a habit. Having a meditation buddy can provide the encouragement and sense of community needed to maintain a regular practice over time.

Summary

Making meditation a habit can have numerous benefits for our physical, mental, and emotional well-being. By taking the time to develop a consistent meditation practice, we can reduce stress, improve focus, and cultivate inner peace and harmony.

To make meditation a habit, it is important to start slowly and set realistic goals. We can also find ways to incorporate meditation into our daily routines, such as practicing in the morning or before bed. Additionally, finding a meditation buddy can provide accountability, motivation, and support to help us maintain our practice over time.

It is important to remember that establishing a consistent meditation practice takes time and dedication. But with patience and persistence, we can develop a habit that supports our overall health and well-being. So I encourage you to start making meditation a habit today, and experience the transformative power of this ancient practice for yourself.

Part VII: Final Thoughts

Meditation is a powerful tool that can help us cultivate inner peace, reduce stress and anxiety, and improve our overall well-being. By taking the time to meditate regularly, we can improve our physical, mental, and emotional health in countless ways.

If you are new to meditation, it can be intimidating to get started. However, it is important to remember that meditation is a practice that anyone can learn and benefit from. Start by setting aside just a few minutes each day to sit quietly and focus on your breath. With time and practice, you can gradually increase the length and frequency of your meditation sessions, and explore different styles of meditation to find what works best for you.

As you begin your meditation practice, it is important to approach it with an open mind and a willingness to learn. Don't be discouraged if you find it difficult to focus or if your mind wanders during meditation. These are common challenges that all meditators face, and with practice, you can develop greater focus and concentration.

Overall, meditation is a valuable tool that can help us lead more peaceful, fulfilling lives. So, I encourage you to start meditating today and discover the many benefits that this practice has to offer.

You have been listening to MEDITATION FOR BEGINNERS: A HOLISTIC APPROACH FOR SELF-IMPROVEMENT, Written by Rosalind Baker, Read for you by {Narrator Name}. Copywrite 2023.